MASTER MINDSET

21 transformative ways to master your life in this uncertain time

---

DIANE DEMETRE

MASTER MINDSET

Copyright © April 2020 Diane Demetre
DIGITAL ISBN: 978-0-6483324-7-3
PRINT ISBN: 978-0-6483324-8-0

ALL RIGHTS RESERVED

No part of this book may be reproduced by any mechanical, photographic or electronic process or in a form of an audio recording, nor may it be stored in a retrieval system, transmitted or otherwise be copied for public or private use—other than for 'fair use' as brief quotations embodied in articles and reviews—without prior written permission of the publisher.

The author of this book does not dispense medical advice or prescribe the use of any technique as a form of treatment for physical, emotional or medical problems without the advice of a physician, either directly or indirectly. The intent of the author is only to offer information of a general nature to help you in your quest for physical, emotional, mental and spiritual well-being. In the event you use any of the information in this book for yourself, the author and the publisher assume no responsibility for your actions.

Contents

About the Author	5
Helpful Hints to Enhance Your Experience	9
Dedication	12
1. What's it all about?	15
Exercise 1	19
2. The Ant Philosophy	21
Exercise 2	24
3. Everything is Energy	29
Exercise 3	38
4. Faith or Fear	44
Exercise 4	49
5. Responsibility is Ours	54
Exercise 5	58
6. Decisions Design Destiny	62
Exercise 6	67
7. Emotional Facet	70
Exercise 7	75
8. Physical Facet	79
Exercise 8	85
9. Mental Facet	88
Exercise 9	93
10. Financial Facet	96
Exercise 10	101
11. Spiritual Facet	104
Exercise 11	109
12. Future Focus	111
Exercise 12	116
13. Gratitude or Grief	119
Exercise 13	123

14. Meditation — Our Natural State of Being	126
Exercise 14	131
15. Parenting as the Presence of Peace	135
Exercise 15	141
16. Imagination, Creativity and Inspiration	145
Exercise 16	150
17. Affirmations and Action	153
Exercise 17	159
18. Keep it Light	162
Exercise 18	167
19. Our Precious Planet	170
Exercise 19	176
20. We are One	180
Exercise 20	185
21. Mastering a Brighter Future	187
Exercise 21	192
Wearing the Crown	195
Dare to be More	199
Award Winning Author	200
Also by Diane Demetre	202

About the Author

Diane Demetre is on a mission to shift human perspective one mind at a time, one business at a time to a Master Mindset, by daring us to be more.

Master Mindset Mentor, Consciousness Coach and Award-winning Author, Diane began her career as a schoolteacher before moving into the entertainment industry, working in television and live theatre, and managing multi-million-dollar productions. Following her onstage career, she spent many years as a stress & life skills therapist, keynote speaker and presenter, and appeared on national radio and television under the pseudonym of the Goddess of Love. A passionate entrepreneur, she's built, owned, and managed thriving national businesses, training over 180 staff in customer service, quality management and leadership prowess. Her successful business, still operating today, has also won numerous quality and business awards.

In *Master Mindset*, Diane shows us how to dare to be more and make that shift from fear to fabulousness in just 21 days, through her powerful messages of hope, awakening, and mastery for humanity. *Master Mindset* was written right in the middle of the global COVID pandemic to empower people in this unprecedented time of isolation and government-imposed restrictions.

Her mantra is to shift our mindset from #Coronavirus to #Consciousness.

The book features key methodologies from her 121 mentoring and group coaching programs, and her highly successful online course The *Master Mindset Method*. Blending key insights from science, psychology, personal empowerment, and spirituality, the knowledge Diane shares is gained from over forty years of teaching, speaking, coaching, counseling, and leading teams of people to master their mindset.

For her outstanding contribution to the arts, Diane was awarded the 2019 SBAA International Women's Day Leader Award for Leadership in the Entertainment, Creative Arts and Media Industry and has been nominated for the Telstra Business Women's Award.

PRAISE FOR MASTER MINDSET

Diane is the voice of reason, rationale, and calm that the world needs. *Now more than ever.* Her no-nonsense approach is precise and succinct yet delivered with Diane's trademark unwavering care and compassion. There are no shortcuts here, Diane's methodical approach will have you exploring your mindset like never before and though challenging at times, the results are undoubtedly expansive and life changing. Master Mindset is *the* guidebook for navigating and emerging from hard times with optimism, empowerment, and belief in yourself. **AusRom Today**

In this inspiring guide to executing strategies to master one's mindset, award-winning author and speaker Demetre explains that implementing a resilient mindset will not only enable a person to show up as their best self at home in isolation while the virus wreaks havoc outside and afterward in the workplace but also an opportunity to transform self-isolation into self-nourishment and self-realization. This motivating work will appeal to self-help readers looking to think outside the box as well as anyone struggling to get by in the current pandemic situation. **Book Sirens Review**

I liken Diane's work to that of Wayne Dyer who has inspired and helped so many around the world. The tools Diane shares are lifelong strategies for creating a life of meaning, connection, and possibility. **Tracy Costa, GradDipPsych (Adv)**

I have been on an awakened spiritual path for a few years now and I loved the honesty and simplicity of this book. It has helped me realign with all that I know to be true, especially with isolation and social distancing. A huge thankyou – this has truly been life changing! I completely understand how to help myself and the planet more clearly now and It is already starting to bring me more of what I want, joy and happiness. **Serenade Publishing**

Helpful Hints to Enhance Your Experience

"Multitasking is a myth. The human brain cannot perform two tasks that require high-level brain function at once. Low-level functions like breathing and pumping blood aren't considered in multitasking. Only the tasks you have to 'think' about are considered. What actually happens when you think you are multitasking is that you are rapidly switching between tasks." Chris Adams, Human Factors Engineer

Before you begin reading this book and each subsequent chapter:

- Eliminate distractions.
- Turn off your phone and other devices.
- Turn off the television and radio.
- Ensure everyone knows you're taking time for yourself, and you don't want to be disturbed.
- Have a notebook and pen to jot down extra

thoughts and ideas. Date each page with the day, month and year.
- Have some coloring pencils close at hand.
- Settle into a comfy reading position.
- If possible, light a candle and some incense.
- Close your eyes, take three deep breaths…
- And now, let's begin with all your focus on YOU!

All truth passes through three stages.
First, it is ridiculed.
Second, it is violently opposed.
Third, it is accepted as being self-evident.

Arthur Schopenhauer

Dedication

Within these pages your conditioned thinking will be challenged, your frame of reference, tested, and hopefully a shift will occur whether you're aware of it or not. I won't present the 'medical or physical' facts relating to the coronavirus pandemic as it cuts its swath across the world. There are many articles written by esteemed professors, doctors and other professionals easily accessible on the internet.

However, I will offer you another perspective. One that if you accept it will transform your life in the present moment. One that will guide you through the anxiety and uncertainty. One that is based in science and spirituality because the two aren't mutually exclusive. And one that will engage, empower, and energize you beyond what you imagined.

It's a perspective I discovered thirty-three years ago when my life crumbled into ruins after I was unfairly sacked when I refused my producer's sexual advances. Though there were no grounds for my dismissal, there were no laws at the time to protect me. And I lost everything. I had no job, no money, no identity, no future, and suicide looked a good option. But in the depths of a devasting depression, a voice whispered, "You are more than what you're demonstrating."

Because of my experience, I understand what you're going through. Though I finally found my way back from the dark night of the soul, I know what it feels like to teeter on the edge of life with all hope gone. When it's so dark, that even with a bright light at the end of the tunnel, you can't find the strength to open your eyes, let alone walk toward it. This is for you. May it guide you Home.

Dare to be more… 🩶

We all have a responsibility to ensure the welfare of humanity, to try to make this a happier more peaceful world.

> His Holiness, The Dalai Lama

ONE

What's it all about?

There are times in our awakening when Life reminds us of who we truly are and why we're here. These reminders are often cloaked in challenging situations, illness and disease, broken relationships, and financial difficulties. They rattle our cage of certainty and comfort, shaking us into the sinking depths of stress, anxiety and depression. Like lost souls drowning in a sea of fear, we cling to the side of our life in desperate panic, kicking and screaming over its demise.

It's at these times of uncertainty and challenge, that we stand on the leading edge of Life, with the opportunity to allow our true Selves to shine forth.

Each of us, at our core, has the same purpose. . . to become fully self-realized. To be someone who is joyously responsible for their reality, has access to their inner resources, treats the world as a friendly place, and is motivated always out of becoming more of who they are. Someone who inspires others through the joy displayed in their own life. Someone who accepts situations the way they are and makes them more, who accepts people the way they are, expecting them to be more.

Our collective purpose is to stop living the dream and wake up. But like our night time dreams, the dream of life as seen through the lens of the limited, human perspective appears real. We're lulled into believing that what's going on is all there is. It's a subtle seduction, and one we've naively accepted all our lives. But within us resides the Truth. That universal, infinite intelligence that knows there's more than what we're currently experiencing and demonstrating. In our hour of need, it beckons to us as whispered words of wisdom. It moves us in a new direction when we've lost our way. And it paints pictures in our mind's eye in our moments of exhaustion. Though this Truth encourages us to wake up, we remain caught in the dream, struggling to open our eyes.

We've all chosen to be here now at this time on the planet, in order to yield into the Truth and be the fullest expression of who we are. To transition, transform and eventually transcend the human experience. We are not victims of this circumstance, we are victorious, if we lean into it with grace and elegance.

Imagine the cycle of the butterfly. After it hatches from the egg, the tiny caterpillar begins growing and expanding rapidly, shedding its skin several times during this stage. Once the caterpillar has reached its full weight and height, it forms into a chrysalis. From the outside, it looks as if the caterpillar may just be resting, but internally unprecedented events are taking place. Inside the chrysalis, the caterpillar is rapidly changing. Old body parts are undergoing a remarkable transformation, called 'metamorphosis,' to become the beautiful parts of the butterfly that will emerge. Tissue, limbs and organs of the caterpillar are all transformed, and by the time it emerges, it does so as an adult butterfly. Though its wings are soft and folded against its body, after resting for a moment, it pumps blood into them, ready to test its wondrous new form. Usually within a three or four-hour period, the butterfly masters flying, and begins its new life.

Consider that we are all butterflies. We are now apparently resting in our chrysalis during our forced isolation. But on the inside, each of us is undergoing monumental change. Our physical, emotional, mental, financial, and spiritual health are transforming in preparation for our emergence into a new life. The old parts of our personality and psyche are being discarded while new, more life-affirming parts are being shaped.

The question is will you fight your transformation and emerge battered and broken with your inherent beauty hidden, unable to spread your wings to soar into a new life? Or will you *yield* into this transformation without resistance, instinctively knowing that there's nothing you need to do but surrender to the natural flow of life. To let go, lean in and let it *be*. And emerge as a new, more beautiful, more successful and more fulfilled version of yourself, ready to take flight into a destiny you not only desire but deserve.

Who will *you* be?

What will you choose?
The Truth will set you free!

EXERCISE:

Spend at least fifteen minutes coloring the below image. As you relax, allow your mind to digest what you've just read. Jot down any thoughts, ideas or realizations you may have. Don't judge, analyze or edit them. Just jot them down.

After you're finished coloring, take the sense of relaxation with you throughout your day. See how long it lasts and if you're aware of when you lose it. Write down how long you remained relaxed here _____

**I am the master of my destiny,
   the captain of my soul.**

> William Ernest Henley

TWO

The Ant Philosophy

Ants never quit.
They think winter all summer.
They think summer all winter.
And ants gather as much as they can.

Ants are clever creatures. They organize the flow of life through hyper-communication; a group consciousness that is plugged into by each individual. Imagine a massive unseen network of pulsing energy, similar to the neural pathways in our brain. This is how the group consciousness connects the insects as one mind relaying messages, signaling alerts and reporting on the welfare of the colony. If the queen ant is spatially separated from her subjects, the building of the colony still proceeds according to some unseen plan. If, however, the queen is killed, all work in the colony stops. No ant knows what to do. Apparently, the queen sends the building plans via the group consciousness of her subjects. Even if she's far away, as long as she's alive, building continues. Bees, termites and other social insects live in societies where the collective power of the colony far outstrips that of the individual and they function with one mind, with one group consciousness for the welfare of the colony.

In humanity's earlier times, we gathered in small colonies and our connection to our group consciousness was necessary for the group's and the individual's survival. But as we developed our separate individuality and no longer needed the protection of the group, we lost touch with the group consciousness and forgot hyper-communication completely. We sacrificed the power and might of a group consciousness, and instead invested in advancing our technology.

The more we delighted in our self-importance, the more selfish we became, and the welfare of the group ranked lower on our priorities. Instead of the universal 'we', we functioned from the personality 'me'. Concerned only for personal gain and not for the greater good, we competed, compared and criticized until we established an 'us' and 'them' mentality, which sanctioned our self-serving individuation further. Striving to achieve absolute authority over our lives and those we could control, we persisted in this limited perspective. While the tenacious, community-minded ants worked tirelessly to bring unity to their colony, we divided and conquered.

Even though as a species we persist with the pursuit of individuation, group consciousness still exists as an invisible network of ever-changing energy. In today's world, we often experience glimpses of this hyper-communication as intuition or inspiration. We're surprised when a friend calls after we were just thinking about them. Or a terrific idea comes to us in the twilight of our sleep.

Unwittingly, we access this energetic network and connect to a vast Consciousness that we're all plugged into but have forgotten because of our mistaken belief that we are separate. Separate from each other, separate from our world and more importantly, we're separate from who we are at a deeper level.

The mass consciousness of the human species, like the group consciousness of the ants is powerful beyond measure. For what we repeatedly think, speak, embody, enact and energize impacts not only ourselves, but our world.

Individually, we manifest our personal reality and collectively we manifest our global reality. From the microcosm, the macrocosm is shaped. Enter coronavirus…

EXERCISE:

Like ants, we too have a philosophy in life. A blueprint we each designed in our formative years on how to view the world and our place in it. Our life philosophy is the foundation stone which underpins our values and beliefs, perceptions, thoughts, feelings and emotions, decisions, actions and habits.

If it's an empowering life philosophy, it supports us. Like the solid, immovable base on which a mighty tower is built, it's the foundation on which enriching values and beliefs, perceptions, thoughts, feeling and emotions, decisions, actions and habits develop, and on which life's rewards pile high.

If it's a disempowering life philosophy, it destabilizes us. We develop unsupportive values and beliefs, perceptions, thoughts, feelings and emotions, decisions, actions and habits. Our life becomes unbalanced, collapses and turns to rubble, leaving us to wonder why.

Most of us are unaware of our life philosophy's existence, much less the enormous influence it has on our lives. If we want the rich rewards life has to offer, we must reengineer our life philosophy, so it fortifies us with strength, integrity and power.

Remember the scene from the movie *Forrest Gump* when Forrest is sitting on a park bench and a nurse sits down beside him. In his innocent, childlike way, he offers her a chocolate. Trying to strike up a conversation, he explains that his mother always said, "Life is like a box of chocolates; you never know which one you're going to get."

In that single sentence, he encapsulates his mother's life philosophy, each candy, each moment or event in life, is a sweet surprise.

For many people, their life philosophy isn't as cheerful or delicious as Forrest's mother's. Some people build their lives on a life philosophy of competition and struggle. Life is like a football game, there's always someone on the other team out to get me. Or life is like a juggling act, there's never enough money to go around. Or on a more positive note, life is like my birthday, every day is filled with lots of presents. Or life is like one big party, happy days and happy people everywhere.

Take some time now to consider what is your life philosophy. Jot down your thoughts here. You may not discover it straight away but over the coming days or weeks, it will become apparent to you as you pay more attention to your thoughts, words, emotions, actions and habits. For if we listen consciously, our life philosophy will tumble from our mouths in the language we use when speaking with our friends, our partners and particularly our family and children. It's there all the time trying to get our attention.

Example: Life is like a box of chocolates; you never know which one you're going to get

Life is like…

_____
_____
_____
_____
_____

Do you think your life philosophy is empowering or disempowering?

_____
_____
_____
_____
_____

Does it help or hinder you? Provide examples

_____
_____
_____
_____
_____

What would be a more empowering philosophy by which to live your life and approach your world? Life is like…

_____
_____
_____
_____
_____

How would a more empowering life philosophy serve you during this time?

_____
_____
_____
_____
_____

Exercise 2

Like the ants, how would it serve your family? What positive changes could it make in your 'colony'?

_____
_____
_____
_____
_____
_____
_____
_____
_____
_____
_____
_____
_____
_____
_____
_____
_____
_____
_____
_____
_____
_____
_____
_____
_____
_____

Everything is energy.
Match the frequency of the reality you want and you cannot help but get that reality.
It can be no other way.
This is not philosophy.
This is physics.

Albert Einstein

THREE

Everything is Energy

We are energetic *beings*. We're not merely flesh, blood and bone with moving parts. Though we've been conditioned to believe that the human body is matter, it's actually energy. We each resonate at a frequency which forms a cohesive pattern of energy to hold a discernable presence, which we then label as a body.

But we don't end at the limits of our skin. We expand four to six feet further as an evermoving, energetic field. These electromagnetic auras can be photographed through Kirlian Camera Imaging. We're not organic bodies with puny personalities living random lives over which we have little control. We are energy in expression, forever creating itself. We are *being*, as a verb, not a noun. And the frequency of energy at which we resonate influences and shapes everything in our lives, and that of others and the planet's.

The power of resonance frequency is witnessed when an opera singer sings a note at the correct pitch and loudness to shatter a crystal glass. This simple, though tricky exercise demonstrates that every physical object has a frequency at which it naturally vibrates and how waves of energy can impinge upon it.

Energy is the fabric of the universe, the essence of life. It's also referred to as God, the Goddess, the Creator, the Universe, Buddha, Knowing, Allah, Creative Mind, Love, the Life Principle, Consciousness and more. And since everything is energy, we too are this energy, individually resonating to our own fluctuating frequency level.

If we stop and consider Einstein's statement long enough, we must conclude that we are not a body with Consciousness. *We are Consciousness with a body*. You are, I am, your partner is, your children are, everyone is Consciousness with a body. We are all one Consciousness, individually and uniquely expressed. There are no exceptions. Either everything is energy, or everything isn't. There are no grey areas in physics. All or nothing.

The fundamental clue to what happens in our life and what is happening in the world is the resonant frequency of our Consciousness, individually and collectively.

As Einstein said, "Match the frequency of the reality you want, and you cannot help but get that reality. It can be no other way."

In other words, *your reality will always match your frequency*. And it is our thoughts, perceptions, beliefs, values, emotions, words and actions that energize our frequency and in turn, color and create our experiences. Think about it this way, if our conditions are *not* controlled by our thoughts, perceptions, beliefs, values, emotions, words and actions, what does control them? Some would say conditions are determined or controlled by circumstances. But what are circumstances? Are they the cause or the effect? Everything we see in our world is the effect. And the cause is our resonance of Consciousness that we each demonstrate in our life. We are the cause.

When unencumbered by our fear-based human perspective—the ego, our resonance of Consciousness vibrates at its purest frequency. This energy paves the way for us to manifest extraordinary lives and businesses. On the other hand, when the ego pervades our Consciousness, this denser resonance is reflected in a life of struggle.

In simple terms, the ego is resistance. It's our reluctance to move forward and embrace the Truth for fear we'll lose our autonomous authority. Think of the ego as a door stop wedged under a door. If we try to open the door, it stops the movement. The more we push against it, the harder it grips until the door is totally jammed. Though it's not as big or strong as the door, it's stubborn and won't budge no matter how much we push against it.

The ego is no more than a stubborn 'door stop' of limiting, fear-based beliefs that we've accepted as being true in our formative years. It's illegitimate. The only power it has over us is the power we give it with our attention. And like the door stop under the door, we mustn't struggle with it, but simply take the pressure off, slide it along out of the way and disregard it.

We mustn't be fooled by the ego's insistence that

what's going on around us in our external world requires all our attention. If the ego hooks us into thinking that it's the *real* us and that our circumstances and conditions are the *real* world, we're in an active state of denying the Truth, which is our indivisibility from Consciousness.

When we disregard the ego, we resonate at a pure frequency of Consciousness and attract extraordinary results such as health, wealth and happiness into our lives. If we don't disregard it, we resonate at a dense frequency of Consciousness and attract miserable results such as poverty, illness and depression.

This is how the law of attraction works and how the coronavirus came into existence. It didn't just come from nowhere because it too is energy.

For at least the past two decades, the energy of arrogance, judgement, prejudice and intolerance has escalated, as witnessed by fear-mongering news reports, social media bullying and a growing segment of the populace who think they have an unalienable right to vilify others for their differences.

Many people have infected themselves with fearful thoughts, perceptions, beliefs, values, emotions, words and actions. They've become so self-important and self-absorbed that they've severed their inherent connection to each other not just as human beings, but as Consciousness in human form.

As a species, we've never been so separated from each other. We've retreated into technology where we mistakenly believe we're more connected, but we're actually more disconnected. Not just from each other, but from our *being*.

In fact, we were self-isolating long before the coronavirus, preferring intimacy with our devices than with each other. We had lost touch with ourselves and our inherent goodness, and in doing so, we manifested our greatest fear. That of not being in control. And chaos is always the result of trying to be in control.

However, at the same time, there's been an underlying energetic push on the planet for awakening. Like the new age movement in the 1980's, there's been a quickening of energy, of Consciousness for us to 'wake up'. To stop dallying in the delusion of three-dimensional life and to transform, transition and transcend to fourth-dimensional reality. This longing for Home has inspired more and more people to practice mindfulness and meditation, and to begin their mission-driven businesses. There's been an urge not just to succeed, but to truly serve others in the process.

Both energies have been at play and the result is the coronavirus—seemingly one of the greatest biological threats that humanity has ever faced or one of the greatest opportunity that's been presented to humanity to awaken.

The law of attraction is sacrosanct and never discriminates. It works perfectly. And since all energy is never inert and expresses itself in form, the virus came into being as the physical manifestation of humanity's burgeoning fear and longing to wake up. From the fear-based perspective, it's manifested from the fear of invasion, fear of immigrants, fear of losing one's way of life, fear that there's not enough to go around, fear of a hostile environment, fear of threat, attack, and finally war. Humanity's hyper communicative energetic network has resonated at such a polluted frequency spreading its tendrils of doom across the globe, that it's manifested the perfect expression of all these fears. Not in the shape of a global war. We have lots of strategies in place to overcome that threat. But in the guise of an unknown and unseen covert enemy. An insidious, little virus loaded with all the fears that have infiltrated humanity for the past two decades.

Conjointly, it's the answer to the prayers for peace and enlightenment. A growing groundswell for social and racial justice, gender equality and conscious living has gained momentum in recent years for humanity to come together as one for the good of all, and the planet. This energetic cry for all-oneness has manifested in the pattern of a brilliantly designed, yet fragile protein molecule which degrades fastest in dehumidified, dry, warm and *bright* environments. Like fear, Covid 19 thrives in the dark. It's the ultimate equalizer of race, gender, social status, religion and financial position, inspiring us to follow Walt Whitman's advice when he wrote, "Keep your face always toward the sunshine and shadows will fall behind you."

Perhaps your intellectual, conditioned thinking is trying to convince you it's more complex than that. That there's nasty things like viruses out there in the world to get you.

"How could *you* be to blame for your ill health?"
"Hell, it's the virus."
"How could *you* be responsible for what's going on?"
"No way. It's the virus' fault."

And so, the ego runs amok, keeping you shackled to a limited human perspective and a life of inertia and misery. The last thing your ego wants you to believe is the Truth.

Everything is energy.

Because the moment you internalize this truth, you're free. Free to think differently, to act differently, to feel differently, to resonate differently and therefore to create a different life.

So, what do we do at this time when the world is overrun by the ego? When well-meaning people are thrusting fear and helplessness upon us from every direction? Despite the external messaging, we do have a choice. We can either lose ourselves and be swallowed up in the terror, or we can shift our perspective to a Master Mindset. Instead of seeing the coronavirus as a disaster, we can see it as the deliverer of renewed hope in a brighter future. We can use isolation as a time to reflect that our families and home life are more important than our jobs and businesses. We can appreciate that love is more important than status. And be grateful for the wake-up call that we must unite to save ourselves, each other and the planet from ignorance. In essence, it's a time of enlightenment to *be* more, individually and collectively.

Henry Ford said, "If you think you can or you can't, you're right."

That's the power of mindset. No matter what you think about yourself—You. Are. Right. Every thought you embody, enact and energize, you make it so. Your mindset will either make or break you, especially through these challenging times and into your future.

Are you just a piece of cosmic dust, a victim of circumstance, a powerless, puny personality with a body of moving parts without any coherent intelligence? Or are you Consciousness with a body? The master of your destiny. The living expression of universal intelligence forever creating itself in perfect harmony through you.

Imagine, if everyone collectively made this shift and affirmed the unalterable Truth, that the only thing going on was the movement of energy, of Consciousness in expression—the entire world situation would change in an instant. We each have the choice to make that happen. We can affirm the Truth, shift our perspective and in turn, influence those around us and the world at large.

The impact of a shift in group consciousness was studied and proven in the 13 Maharishi Effect study published in 2003. The study demonstrated how organized, regular transcendental meditation in 24 US control cities reduced crime rates in those cities. In some cases, by as much as 16%. This study broadened its scope to England, India, Israel and Canada and in each case, crime rates fell when the transcendental meditation group exceeded the square root of 1% of the population.

Studies such as these demonstrate time and again that the mind, our Consciousness has the power to affect not just the individual, but the collective.

Everything is energy. Match the frequency of the reality you want, and you cannot help but get that reality. It can be no other way. This is not philosophy. This is physics.

Since what we *repeatedly* think, embody, enact and energize, we become and *then attract*, now is the time to shift our perspective—from panic to peace, from coronavirus to consciousness, and from fear to faith in ourselves. It's time to consciously harness the energy of change and master our destiny.

There's never been a better time to *be* all you came here to be.

EXERCISE:

Shifting to a Master Mindset is not so much about what we do or have. It's about who we're *being*, particularly during these uncertain and unnerving times.

So, who will you need to *be* in order to *do* what it takes to *have* the reality you desire most? Because if you're not currently living that reality, you're going to have to make some changes and resonate to a purer frequency of Consciousness. You're going to have to *be* more. Make a list of the qualities of your new empowered state of *being.* Write at least 50!

For example: I am strong, I am compassionate, I am peaceful, I am creative, I am confident, I am intelligent...

I am:

_____
_____
_____
_____
_____
_____
_____
_____
_____
_____
_____
_____
_____
_____
_____
_____

As you continue through this book, add to your list. Refer to it often. The more you empower your new state of being, the more you connect with *being*.

Now it's time to reflect on what *is* the reality you want. You must get clear on what it looks like, where it is, who's there with you. How does your ideal day start? Be specific. What happens during the day until you finally go to sleep at night? Take some time to write down your ideal day from start to finish, allowing your imagination to spill onto the page.

My Ideal Day

_____
_____
_____
_____
_____
_____
_____
_____
_____
_____
_____
_____
_____
_____
_____
_____
_____
_____

Exercise 3

Exercise 3

Now that you've mapped out who you're going to *be* and the reality you want, you must resonate to the frequency of *that reality today.* You must match the frequency of *that reality*, and not what appears to be going on around you. Shift your perspective and in turn, your reality and results will change.

Energize your new state of *being* by embodying and enacting your *I am* qualities. Use them as your new self-talk mantra instead of self-criticism. Stand in front of the mirror, look at yourself with love and repeat them over and over.

Teach your children by your example. Invite them to join you in front of the mirror and together repeat your new self-nourishing mantra until it's anchored into your mind, body and soul.

Embody, enact and energize your new empowered state of *being* in every thought, word and action. Remind each other often of who you truly are. Call yourself and each other to a higher standard with the energy of love.

Remember, you are *Consciousness with a body.*

You are the Master of your destiny and the Captain of your soul.

Dare to *be* more of you <u>now</u>.

Faith is taking the first step even when you don't see the whole staircase.

Martin Luther King, Jr.

FOUR

Faith or Fear

At this time more than ever before we must not believe everything we see and hear, for it will only amplify the energy of fear in ourselves and the planet. Perspective has never been more important. The 2009 swine flu infected 1.4 billion people around the world and killed 575,000 people. There was no media panic and societies didn't shut down. Going into April 2020, Coronavirus has infected 1,924,635 people and 119,686 people have died, most of who had pre-existing conditions. Though well-intentioned, are the draconian laws of removing our basic freedoms, policing people in parks and locking entire populations away in their homes for an undisclosed period of time the best course of action? Or are they merely a knee-jerk reaction by governments to escalating fear and damning public opinion which will give them time to impose new containment strategies?

Because of the collective, misguided belief in separateness and mortality, our fear of death is greater than our love of life. Rather than perpetuating the horror of dying, shouldn't we be encouraging everyone to live well? Infected not so much by a tiny virus, but by the much larger contagion of fear, we've retreated further into the ego, and the divisive 'us' and 'them' mentality. Perhaps the world needs to take a collective breath and reconsider. Is minimising the deaths of some worth sacrificing the economic, social and mental stability of many for possibly generations to come?

Though we have little alternative but to comply with governmental restrictions, we do have the power to choose our perspective on absolutely everything, each moment of every day. We can approach life from the fear-based human perspective, the ego, or from a faith-based Master Mindset. Not the religious kind of faith, but the transformative energy that has the power to change everything.

Faith is a definite mental attitude accompanied by a focus within that's enhanced by meditation. It's knowing without doubt or fear that everything will work out for the best. And the world could certainly use a bit more of this kind of faith at present. If we live with faith, knowing that nothing is too good to be true, nothing is too wonderful to happen, and nothing is too good to last, we can be buffeted by the winds of change, and instead of being dashed against the rocks, we align our sails and set a better course.

Faith can be likened to wearing a pair of glasses, when viewing a stunning spring day. Mother Nature is in her glory with brilliant blue skies, the greenest grass, a gentle stream trickling clean and pure down the hillside, and fields of perfumed flowers through which wildlife scamper. Unfortunately, most of us view this perfect spectacle through dirty, finger-smudged glasses. The image we see is distorted and less vibrant, and so we feel uneasy and restless. However, what we see doesn't reflect the true beauty and perfection of the landscape. It's merely our misperception of it. Over time, we come to believe in this inaccurate representation of the landscape. And for many of us, this is how we're viewing our world at the moment, though dirty, smudged glasses.

Three options exist for us to see clearly. The first is to leave our glasses in place and rub at the lenses in the hope this will clean them enough for us to enjoy the view. This is referred to as insanity—doing the same thing over and over again but expecting to see different results.

The second option is to remove the glasses and clean them thoroughly before resetting them onto our face—this is the process of correction, compliance and conditioning, of doing something different but still from the same limited perspective as before.

The third option is a leap of faith, where we simply grow tired of the view we're experiencing and throw the glasses away altogether. Sick and tired of being sick and tired, we leap from who we are to who we want to be, without any safety net, except faith in ourselves. That leap of faith provides sparkling clarity because it fast-tracks us to our *being* where we discover we didn't need the glasses in the first place.

Just as we can't see the beauty of the landscape if the glasses remain dirty, we can't demonstrate both fear and faith in our lives at once, because one contradicts the other. The stronger of the two produces the results. Because the law of attraction is an energetic law, the results we currently have in our life demonstrate whether we live predominantly with the energy of faith or fear. Faith brings success, while fear brings failure.

Faith isn't complicated. It's a conscious choice; a great adventure and stimulating opportunity to use the higher laws of Consciousness for definite purposes. And like any skill, it's best tested and strengthened on life's smaller challenges, so it's up to the task in times of greater difficulties. Currently, humanity is undergoing a major test of faith, though most don't recognize it as such. Having to deal with forced isolation, the risk of contracting coronavirus, the loss of income and possible long-term unemployment is terrifying for most people. Their faith reserves are on empty, and they've succumbed to fear. Fear can be simplified as false evidence appearing real. Like everything, fear is an energy. When we live in fear, we attract the evidence of fear in our reality. What we resist, persists, and if we're fearful of being infected, it then follows that we'll attract that into our reality.

Whereas those who succeed at anything in life are fearless in their faith in themselves and that they will succeed. It's not that they don't experience fear, it's that they inherently know that their *faith is stronger than their fears*. They also know that fearlessness is not the absence of fear but going beyond fear. They grit their teeth and press on with formidable faith while others drown in their fear.

Fear is the worst enemy of all, for fear attracts fear,

whereas faith expels fear. The fearless, unfettered mind, the mind filled with faith, attracts only good. If we are to emerge from this pandemic victorious, we must withdraw our faith in the ego and reinvest it into our *being*. We must believe fervently in ourselves and our mission on earth and know, unequivocally that it will come to pass. Why? Because as we believe so it will be done. Whether we want to accept the law of attraction or not, it's a proven energetic law of the universe. Our reality is the result of our energy.

The more faith we have, the more trust we build. Trust in ourselves, trust in our *being*, trust in knowing that our faith will carry us through. Trust and faith are powerful partners and are precursors to revelations that cannot be imagined by critical thinking. But until we practice faith and trust, we'll never know. And now is the time find out. The more we stop, sit and contemplate the energy of faith and trust rising within ourselves, the better equipped we'll be to face the times ahead.

There is a space within each of us between what we cannot see and what we believe, across which we leap. Everyone is being called upon at this time, to leap. To disregard the ego and have faith and trust in ourselves that we are more than what we're demonstrating. That there is more to life than we ever imagined. It's the time to lean into this Truth with all our might and believe!

EXERCISE:

On a scale from 1 to 5 being the highest, how would you rate your level of faith in the current coronavirus situation? _____

Tick off whichever bullet points from either column best identifies your perspective in life.

Human Perspective is turned outwards with a primary focus on the external world	**Master Mindset** is turned inwards with a primary focus on the internal world
• Information • Knowledge • Conditions • Circumstances • Fear-based decisions • Negative Emotions • Doing • Having • Striving • Achievement • Comparison • Competition • Judgement • Anxiety • Stress • Inertia • Depression • Death	• Wisdom • Self-knowing • Conscious • Personal empowerment • Faith-based decisions • Love-based feelings • Creativity • Gratitude • Elegance • Fulfilment • Service • Grace • Compassion • Joy • Peace • Momentum • Growth • Transformation
React to circumstances	Respond to circumstances
Disempower myself	Empower myself
Live my life from Ego	Live my life from *Being*

Tally up the ledger. Are you predominantly fear-based or faith-based? _____

Do you predominantly live from the human perspective or a Master Mindset?_____

Our faith grows when we embrace the valuable lessons of perseverance, endurance, steadfastness, detachment, character, service, love, compassion, trust, humility and patience.

On a scale from 1 to 5, how would you rate your faith based on these qualities?

1	2	3	4	5
Low	Below Average	Average	Good	Excellent

	1	2	3	4	5
Perseverance					
What more can you **be** or **do** to make it a 5?					
Endurance					
What more can you **be** or **do** to make it a 5?					
Steadfastness					
What more can you **be** or **do** to make it a 5?					
Detachment from the ego					
What more can you **be** or **do** to make it a 5?					
Character					
What more can you **be** or **do** to make it a 5?					
Service to others					
What more can you **be** or **do** to make it a 5?					
Love					
What more can you **be** or **do** to make it a 5?					
Compassion					
What more can you **be** or **do** to make it a 5?					
Trust					
What more can you **be** or **do** to make it a 5?					
Humility					
What more can you **be** or **do** to make it a 5?					
Patience					
What more can you **be** or **do** to make it a 5?					

Don't fear the shift you're experiencing. The more you identify with Consciousness, with your *being*, the less influence fear will have over you.

Remember, fear can be **F**orgot **E**verything **A**nd **R**un or **F**ace **E**verything **A**nd **R**ise. The choice is yours.

Lean into the experience of faith, rather than resist it. It's merely a transition in which your attachment to what you thought was real is falling away. Hold firm to your new empowered state of *being* for it will add more strength, flexibility and power to your faith muscles and in turn, your reality will reflect this.

**You must take personal responsibility.
You cannot change the circumstances,
the seasons or the wind,
but you can change yourself.**

Jim Rohn.

FIVE

Responsibility is Ours

Each of us lives a life of our own making. Nothing ever happens to us by chance. And nothing happens to us because we deserve to suffer. The old saying that everything happens for a reason tends to absolve us from being responsible for our lives. There's a reason that everything happens—the reason is us.

Because we act like energetic transmitters, attracting to us similar energy in the form of people and experiences, we are each responsible for our reality. Nothing happens to us that we didn't first influence in some way. What we think, speak, perceive, believe, embody, enact and energize repeatedly returns to us, like for like. We cannot demonstrate in the world of effects (our physical life) beyond what our current world of causes (our Consciousness) embodies. Though uncomfortable as this seems, we are living a life of our choosing.

But you say, "I didn't choose for the coronavirus to change my way of life?"

But you do have a choice in the present moment as

to how you *respond* to your changed personal reality because of the pandemic. You can choose to suffer or thrive, to retreat or rise. You can react from the fear-based human perspective or respond from a faith-based Master Mindset. Either way, you'll reap reciprocal results.

If we're experiencing pain, it's because we're resisting change. We're valuing our problems over the opportunity to enlighten our Consciousness. Like a child whose feet are growing too big for their shoes, the global Consciousness is stretching and groaning as if awakening from a long slumber. Our role isn't to try and squeeze ourselves back into shoes that no longer fit, into our old life. Our role is to discard our old shoes, our old perspective and be willing to grow into a new life.

As Viktor Frankl wrote, "When we are no longer able to change the situation, we are challenged to change ourselves."

And the impact of the coronavirus is certainly challenging us to change from being reactive to being responsible for every facet of our lives.

Being responsible doesn't mean to take on duties and obligations for another, because no one can be responsible for another. Responsibility means the ability to respond to a situation and not blame someone else, a circumstance or a condition.

Refusing to take responsibility and be accountable for one's actions is why few people excel in their lives. Personal shame turns to blame, and guilt turns to judgement because of a lack of self-responsibility. These small-minded, limited emotions stunt our Consciousness and produce small, limited results. However, the more we practice being responsible for ourselves and our lives, the more conscious we become, and the more we govern a destiny that we desire most.

One of the most pervasive myths in western culture today is that we're *entitled* to a great life. That somehow, somewhere, someone is responsible for supplying us with a life of health, wealth and happiness. But the truth is that there's only one person responsible for the quality of the life we live. Us! If we want to create the reality we desire most, we must take responsibility for everything that we experience in life. But most of us operate from a limited human perspective and continue to blame something outside of ourselves for the parts of our life we don't like. We blame our parents, our boss, our friends, our colleagues, our clients, our spouse, the weather, the economy, the government, our lack of money and now the coronavirus—anyone or anything we can pin the blame on. We never want to look at where our reality begins—with us.

While we blame other people for the misery multiplying in our lives we're caught in the dense energetic frequency of fear. We react to the world based on the ego's fear-based perspective, and spend our days frustrated, impatient and stressed. But we have the choice to shift our perspective and resonate to a purer frequency of Consciousness at any time.

Because of our current enforced solitude, we stand at the threshold of recognizing reality more clearly than ever before—a personal reality we're responsible for. Though this may be confronting, there's no blame to lay, particularly not on ourselves. For guilt is another of the ego's strategies to stop us from transformation. We all did the best we could with the information we had. Now we can do better.

That we are each responsible for our personal reality is a liberating realization, for it means we have power. Power to change our thoughts, perceptions, beliefs, values, emotions, words and actions by being responsible. But it's up to each of us to use this time wisely and not join the pity party. We must abandon our old limiting belief of just needing to survive and instead, decide to thrive.

Like newly planted seeds in the garden, we've been given a rare opportunity to grow, to energize ourselves, elevate our minds and flourish. We mustn't squander our isolation on mindless nonsense. The sooner we realize that we can't escape the responsibility of tomorrow by evading it today, the sooner we will prosper.

EXERCISE:

The process of shifting our perspective to being responsible is softened by willingness. Willingness is the ability to see everything, everyone and every situation brand new. When we're willing to shift our perspective, we relax, and in that calmer energy we're able to respond. Without willingness, we become tense and there appears to be sacrifice. But the concept of sacrifice is a function of the ego as it tries to seduce us into believing that we've given up something in order to grow, to expand our Consciousness. The ego is terrified that it will be the sacrifice. That we will no longer need it. But this idea is but another misperception. Since there is only one thing going on which is Consciousness in expression and the ego is illegitimate, then there's nothing to sacrifice. All that's needed to be responsible is the willingness to be responsible.

We must remember that being self-responsible isn't about blaming ourselves or finding fault in our actions. It's about unleashing our power to change, to shift and resonate to a purer frequency of Consciousness. When we're being responsible we're unburdened of our guilt.

Seven Key Questions:

1. Are you willing to respond to your world rather than react to it?

   _____

2. Are you willing to give up the shame and guilt for not having done it better?

   _____

3. Are you willing to take responsibility for *every* facet of your life?

   _____

4. Are you willing not to blame someone else, a circumstance or condition?

   _____

5. Are you willing to be accountable for your results?

   _____

6. Are you willing to no longer make excuses why your life isn't working?

   _____

7. Are you willing to be responsible?

   _____

List three recent situations where you've reacted and write down how you could have responded to produce better outcomes.

_____
_____
_____
_____
_____
_____
_____
_____
_____
_____
_____
_____

As you become more responsible, your reality will change accordingly. You'll want to share your new-found wisdom with others who may or may not care. Remember, you're not responsible for the receptiveness of others. Everyone finds their own way Home, and no one does it the same as anyone else. Be content to walk your own path.

**We all make choices,
but in the end our choices make us**

Ken Levine

SIX

Decisions Design Destiny

Since all thought is energy and has power in our lives, then all decisions are likewise powerful. They possess catalytic value for turning our dreams into reality, but it's up to us to harness the power within ourselves and take action. There's virtually nothing we can't do once we make a committed, congruent decision and embody it through action.

But what is a congruent decision? It's the one we make with our heart, not our head. That intuitive, gut instinct that nudges us, pointing in one direction or the other. When we dare to make decisions based on what our heart or gut tells us, we challenge the conditioned thinking we've been taught to value, and in doing so, we're more likely to shift our perspective, ignore past limitations and external influences, and press on.

For every decision we make, whether consciously or habitually sets the direction and destination for our life. Each decision sets in motion the cause which produces an effect in our reality. The great thing about decision-making is that we can change our destiny at any time by making new, congruent decisions.

Our thoughts, perceptions, beliefs, values, emotions, words and actions form the road map for our lives. If we enrich them, our experience likewise will become enriched. The moment we make congruent, inspired decisions in alignment with our *being*, we open the super highway to this reality.

If we want a better-quality life, we must think better-quality thoughts, ask better-quality questions, make better-quality decisions and take better-quality actions. Instead of asking the victim question of "Why is this happening to me?" we need to be asking better-quality questions.

How can I change to get a better outcome?
What am I willing to do to make myself better?
How can I move on?
What is this situation teaching me?

While we focus on the external events and ask disempowering questions, we fail to register that though there may appear to be multiple choices in life, there are only two motivators of those choices—love or fear.

For example, in the current coronavirus climate we're being asked to practice social distancing. One person may comply to the request out of love for themselves and other people. They remain at a safe distance because they're wanting to do the right thing and believe that distance is positive to their health and to others. Another person may comply, however they're motivated to keep their distance out of fear. They're terrified that if they get too close, they'll catch the virus. They keep their distance because they're scared that others may be carriers of the contagion and want to safeguard themselves.

In both cases the action is the same, compliance with social distancing, but the energy behind the motivation is diametrically opposed. Love or fear. Since everything is energy, and our reality matches our frequency, which of these two people are more likely to contract coronavirus? It's simple physics when viewed from this frame of reference.

That's not to say we should abandon all common sense. On the contrary, common sense supports us in our movement forward with a Master Mindset. When we feel uneasy and aren't quite ready for the next shift, we can use common sense as a fall-back position until we summon up more faith to fortify ourselves for our advance. But once we understand that every decision we make, whether inconsequential or life-changing, is motivated by love or fear, we're able to make more conscious, congruent decisions.

Equipped with this understanding, we can align our decisions with our *being*, knowing that we'll never be led astray. Clarity replaces chaos and certainty replaces confusion. And all it takes is practice.

Start with the small decisions first. Before you make any decision, stop and become conscious that you're in decision-making mode. Perhaps it's to go to the fridge to get a snack, to put on a movie, to wash clothes or make dinner.

Check in and ask, "Is it appropriate for me to do this now?"

Wait, tune it and then act on your gut instinct or failing that, your common sense. If you know that the action you're about to take is motivated by fear, anger, frustration, resentment, guilt, apathy, bitterness or shame—stop. Choose differently!

One of the greatest freedoms we have is the right to make our own free will decisions. And with this right comes the extraordinary power to change our lives or not. If we continue making unconscious, fear-motivated decisions, our lives will deteriorate. Even when we make no decision in a situation, we are choosing not to decide. We can't escape the fact that life is a series of choices we make on a moment by moment basis, and that those decisions design our destiny. We must know exactly what that destiny is, match its energetic frequency and then make decisions that energize that destiny into reality.

There are a couple of important decisions to make right at this moment.

Are you going to *be* who you and your family need to transition through this time?

_____
_____
_____
_____
_____
_____
_____
_____

Describe the new empowered you.

Do you have the determination, discipline and drive to *be* that person?

Are these qualities on your *I am* list?

EXERCISE:

Consider the major decisions you've made in your life. Which ones were love-based, and which were motivated out of fear?
List some below, identifying the motivators.

_____
_____
_____
_____
_____
_____
_____
_____
_____
_____
_____

Knowing what you now know, what you would tell your younger self?

_____
_____
_____
_____
_____
_____
_____
_____
_____
_____
_____

Do you have a new approach to decision-making? If so, what is it and how will it assist you in making better decisions?

Your emotions are the slaves to your thoughts, and you are the slave to your emotions.

Elizabeth Gilbert

SEVEN

Emotional Facet

Our emotional nature is intrinsically tied to our physicality, our mental health, and our spiritual and financial well-being. These five facets resonate and form the cohesive pattern of energy that make us unique. Just as well-engineered infrastructure keeps the integrity of a building sound, so too do the five facets influence the integrity of our *being*.

If we resonate at a pure frequency of Consciousness, this will be reflected in our emotional, physical, mental, financial, and spiritual good health. If we resonate at a dense frequency of Consciousness because we're caught in the ego's limited human perspective, we'll suffer poor emotional, physical, mental, financial and spiritual health. Therefore, it's in our best interest, particularly now as the world undergoes a seismic shift to ensure we're energizing these facets to the purest frequency of Consciousness we possibly can.

Feelings such as happiness, faith, passion, trust, kindness, tenderness, empathy, sympathy, honesty, and compassion have their origins in love—love for oneself and love for others. Anger, resentment, victimhood, deceit, martyrdom, frustration, apathy, bitterness, guilt, shame, and jealousy are fear-based—fear of loss, fear of not being good enough, and fear of being less than or greater than. In simple terms, emotions are the ego's reaction to life while feelings are our *being's* response to life.

Fear-based emotions are nothing more than energy suppressed at the time of expression. They're not a life sentence, but merely a lesson in love and forgiveness. These fear-based emotions and the beliefs on which they precariously balance were constructed throughout our life, beginning in our formative years. For example, there were times when we were manipulated by our parents to do something that we didn't want to do, and we felt resentful or angry, but we weren't allowed to express this energy. We had to bottle it up and comply with our parents' wishes. If we'd chosen to express this energy at the time, we probably would've done so by imitating the unacceptable behaviors of those around us which would've gotten us into even more trouble.

We also suppressed fear-based emotions because of our education system, with its rules and prescribed conformity. Individuality or enlightened thinking wasn't something that most education systems encouraged or supported. If we were different to the norm, we were controlled into compliance.

Likewise, society and religion are organized for the purpose of containment and eliminating the extremes. Trapped within these parameters, we may feel ourselves oppressed and suppressed. Added to this, is the collective unconscious where competition is revered and a win-lose mentality seeps into our psyche. This emotional energy, suppressed at the time of its expression, clings to us waiting to be expressed. If we don't free this energy, it leads to a disposition of hostility. An energy which has claimed its place high on the planet's rankings for years. Hostility feeds the ego and becomes a vicious energetic downward spiral. When directed outward it expresses itself as blame and judgement and when directed inward, we experience it as negative self-talk, self-denial and self-destruction.

Then there is the most subtle and demoralizing of all fear-based emotions—not feeling good enough. Without the recognizable fervor of anger, frustration, grief or indignation, it creeps in and leaves us with a sense of stagnation, despair and dread. It's one of the most significant yet obscure conditions underlying the human condition. Like the root of all evil, it's buried within each of us, spreading its tendrils deeper, sucking the goodness out of us.

Not feeling good enough comes in various guises. It haunts and attacks us when our life is working—when we're making the changes, when things are working, when we're creating our destiny, we still feel an undefinable stress. Or it cloaks itself in guilt, shame, depression, and issues of deservedness which lead to self-sabotage and self-punishment. It doesn't make sense why we're feeling these fear-based emotions, but still they lurk in the background of our daily life. Many times, not feeling good enough arrives and leave us with a sense of despair or dread, and we don't know why. There's no good reason. But the worst is that left unabated, it produces lethargy and apathy, and we just don't care. We curl up in a ball of stagnation and even though we know the steps to take, we don't take them. We feel overwhelmed and slide further into the depths of this negative emotion, trying to validate our failures with excuses such as… "I guess I'm not good enough, not smart enough, not pretty enough or lucky enough to live the life I want."

This pity-party is a dead end because there's no value in suffering.

That's not to say we shouldn't allow ourselves a jolly good cry. Crying acts as a release valve cleansing our energetic field, while biologically there's a stress hormone called cortisol that's concentrated in our tears. We literally cry out our stress. When you find yourself on the bathroom floor crying, validate the emotion and resist judging yourself for the experience.

Be gentle with yourself and allow the emotion its expression. If possible, channel the energy into affirming what you *do* want, and not what you don't want. Instead of proclaiming how unhappy you are or that you can't cope; instead voice your desire for the future and how you want your life to be. It may feel a little strange when you do this, but this simple shift minimizes the anguish and energizes your faith in a fulfilling future.

There's another alternative to releasing our emotional past. Instead of diving headfirst into the dumpster of our suppressed emotional past and ferreting around in our garbage, we can transmute this suppressed energy with love. Love and forgiveness free us to have dominion in our lives, rather than trying to dominate our lives and everyone in it. Feeling love for ourselves, each other and the world at large develops positive, empowering emotional patterns and enlightens us of fear.

All disease comes from a state of fear, from fear-based emotions left to fester. Healing is essentially a release of fear. Therefore, the more love-based feelings we experience in our lives, the more love we give, receive and *be*; the more we are healed. More correctly, the more of who we truly are as *being* is revealed. If ever there was a miracle cure, the energy of love is it.

It may take a little practice to choose faith and love in instances that make you want to scream. But walk away and take three deep breaths. Instead of suppressing the energy, channel it and transmute it. Resonate at a purer frequency of Consciousness, know that you can *be* more and respond from a more empowered perspective.

EXERCISE:

Realize that in every situation, whether you're experiencing energy-in-motion as loving feelings or fear-based emotions, the energy is yours. No one else's. We've been conditioned to blame someone else for how we feel. However, they didn't come along, flip open our heads and pour a jug of loving feelings or fear-based emotions down our throat. Therefore, no one is to blame. It's no one's fault. And, it's not our fault either. It's just energy wanting to be expressed and transmuted as quickly as possible, so it no longer clouds our energetic field. This is when the Truth Process comes in handy.

Here's an example. You've arranged to meet your husband at a certain time at the shopping center. You're there as planned, but he's not. You text him and he answers he's on his way. Your energy begins to boil with frustration. Fifteen minutes, and he's still not there. Another text. He apologizes, he got delayed. By now, you're furious and your energy is white hot. You begin the blame game.

I feel angry because he

_____
_____
_____

I feel worthless because he

_____
_____
_____

I feel rejected because he

_____
_____
_____

In order to transmute this energy, you take responsibility and complete the Truth Process.

I feel angry because I

_____
_____

I feel worthless because I

_____
_____

I feel rejected because I

_____
_____

Perhaps your answers really are:
I feel angry because I can't control my husband.
I feel worthless because I'm always giving up my needs for everyone else.
I feel rejected because I allow this behavior to continue.

Once we consciously apply the Truth Process to any situation where fear-based emotions threaten to overwhelm us, we can then respond, shift our mindset and resonate at a purer frequency of Consciousness. The Truth does set us free!

Exercise 7

Make a list of every loving feeling or fear-based emotion you experienced in the last twenty-four hours. Next to it write how you could energize that feeling to a purer resonance.

For example:
When I woke up, I felt okay, but if I'd taken a couple of minutes before rushing to start my day and feeling stressed, I would've been happier.
I lost my temper with my son which I felt bad about. I should've stopped and taken a couple of deep breaths before losing it.

_____
_____
_____
_____
_____
_____
_____
_____

Jot down loving feelings you wished you'd experienced and how you can energize them to be part of your next day.

_____
_____
_____
_____
_____
_____
_____

**Take care of your body.
It's the only place you have to live.**

> Jim Rohn

EIGHT

Physical Facet

Since everything is energy, it means that our body demonstrates our resonant frequency of Consciousness at every moment in our lives. Better than any medical book, it tells us what we need to know to improve our health. Resonate at a pure frequency of Consciousness and demonstrate outstanding health. Resonate at a dense frequency of Consciousness and our bodies try to get our attention. These messages come as little niggling sensations, whispers such as cold or stiffness of the joints or a small injury. Whispers remind us that we're not resonating at our purest frequency of Consciousness. If we ignore these whispers, they'll turn into shouts, screaming at us, while discomfort and disease run rampant through our bodies.

Any deformity, dissonance, disease or distress we experience is because we have chosen a disempowering belief or attitude about our bodies. Since our bodies aren't organic material, but pure energy, the experience of imperfection is illegitimate. We're not stuck with the apparent 'imperfection', because our bodies aren't governed by the laws of matter. They're governed by energetic laws.

Einstein said, "Reality is merely an illusion. Albeit, a very persistent one."

Imagine a square piece of vinyl. It's energy resonates at a frequency which holds it in a discernable, cohesive pattern of a square. If we were to push our fist into the vinyl, the pressure distorts its shape. The same is true for our physical body. When we criticize, depreciate, abuse and use it as a defense against our world, we apply pressure to its discernable presence. The pattern of energy becomes dense, doesn't flow freely, and we force our bodies out of shape and into dis-ease.

In the example of the vinyl square, the moment we remove our fist and relieve the pressure, it returns to its original shape, it's original pattern of energy. Likewise, when we relieve the pressure and stress, and stop using our bodies as a shield; healing occurs. Healing isn't about having a creative idea on how we'd like to look, have to look or are forced to look. It's about abandoning those ideas, appreciating and loving our body, being undefended against it and experiencing Consciousness expressing itself in its perfection. Or more correctly, healing is revealing the true nature of the energy which constitutes our body.

That's not to say we should refuse medical assistance when needed. We must all function within our comfort zones and not cross a threshold that moves us into fear, because fear will only force our bodies further out of shape. But it does mean that we're each responsible for our health and at no time should we give our power away to another person, no matter their credentials. Our inner self-knowing is the supreme healer.

Since we're embodied consciousness, we have a responsibility to honor and value our bodies—to care for, love and provide our embodiment with the nutrients, exercise, hydration and restorative sleep needed to function most effectively. If we respect our car enough to fuel it with the correct octane, check the air in the tires and service it regularly, surely our bodies are worthy of the same attention.

With movable joints, our bodies are made for action, not to slouch inactively in front of electronic screens or on couches, hour after hour. The adage of "use it or lose it" is never more relevant than when applied to the physical body. Research in recent years has illustrated the outstanding benefits of exercise in reducing the risk of dementia, slowing aging, protecting and improving brain function, and promoting psychological health and good mood. The consequences of a sedentary life are as well documented as they are grim. People with low levels of physical activity are at higher risk of worsening back pain, depression and anxiety and of early death by many different kinds of cancer, heart disease and Alzheimer's disease.

It's not that we don't know this, it's that we don't act on it. And if the coronavirus is teaching us anything, it's showing us that anyone with a pre-existing health condition is at an increased risk of infection. So, whether it's a stick or the carrot that gets us off the couch during our isolation, let's move!

Remaining properly hydrated is crucial to our physical health and brain function. It's the best nutrient of all as it detoxifies, aids in exercise recovery, hydrates the skin and tissues and increases metabolism. Eight glasses a day keeps the doctor away.

Then there's our ultimate life-sustaining, preventive measure—our breath. The power of conscious breathing has long been extolled in yoga and meditation practices as a super pathway to support our sympathetic and parasympathetic systems, ensuring healthy physiological responses. Filling our lungs deeply and controlling the rhythm of the breath increases the oxygen permeation in our blood vessels, which in turn reduces inflammation throughout our body. When we energize ourselves with conscious deep breathing, we resonate at a purer frequency of Consciousness, cleanse our bodies and create an internal environment less likely to foster infection.

Though many don't realize it sleep deprivation can have serious short and long-term consequences on their health including delayed reaction times, glucose levels, mood, headaches, impaired memory and focus, and hormone imbalances. Not enough restorative sleep has been shown to shrink the brain. The way your brain processes information, consolidates memories, makes connections and clears out toxins, suffers when you deprive it of healthy, deep sleep. Improving your sleep habits improves your brain and in turn, your mindset.

Living healthy, healthful lives is our birthright.

Excusing ourselves from being healthy by blaming our genes, circumstances or conditions is an erroneous, disempowering belief. Deepak Chopra, M.D., and Rudolph E. Tanzi, Ph.D., co-authors of *Super Genes: Unlock the Astonishing Power of Your DNA for Optimum Health and Well-Being* demonstrate how we shape our gene activity and how genes act as a tool for personal transformation. "Everything you do, every choice you make, whether it is a good habit or a bad habit, is changing your genetic activity." According to the authors, optimizing our gene expression will not only positively affect our life, but also the course of human evolution. "Genes hold the past, the present, and the future of life on this planet." When we polish the physical facet by honoring our bodies, we align our bodies with our *being*, and we begin to sparkle.

As far back as 1985, neuroscientist Dr Candace Pert published ground-breaking research showing that feelings and emotions can trigger peptides to carry chemical messages throughout the body and chemically change the cells in the body. Her research demonstrated that the mind and the body are not separate, and we cannot treat one without the other. Yet so many people still think that disease is random. They believe some people are blessed with good health, while some are not. Yet it has been proven that we influence our health on all levels. The difference between these two groups of people is their *mindset*.

Since we are Consciousness with a body, it behooves each of us not to fall into fear during the coronavirus crisis for we will surely change the chemical messages in our body and become more susceptible to that which we fear—infection.

The body is a remarkable operating system and when we nourish our energetic physiology by listening, complying and acting on its intuitive instructions, it responds in kind by emanating unblemished health.

EXERCISE:

Since there are all sorts of free online exercise and movement classes available, there's no excuse not to move during isolation. Find classes that you like and schedule to do at least twenty to thirty minutes of exercise, five times a week at the same time. Ritualizing the class at the same time every day makes it easier to do. Expect your ego to bombard you with lots of excuses as to why you can't do the class…your kids, your partner, your work, your parents, your dog. But this is *your* physical facet and if you don't value you, how can you expect anyone to value you. I know this might sound a little harsh, but a life bursting with good physical health is your birthright. Claim it and move that body.

Use the below table as a 30-day calendar for your next month's exercise schedule. List the type of exercise and the time you spent exercising for each day

Exercise 8

Below is a powerful authorization which will help you energize your body to express its perfect health. Speak this often with unwavering faith and a deep knowing that you are indeed Consciousness in a body.

I authorize my body to release whatever is not necessary to its perfect functioning, and I withdraw all prior conscious and unconscious authorizations to the contrary.

**If you are facing a new challenge or being asked to do something that you have never done before don't be afraid to step out.
You have more capability than you think you do but you will never see it unless you place a demand on yourself for more.**

Joyce Meyer

NINE

Mental Facet

Like everything, thoughts are energy. They're the energetic movement of the Consciousness we currently embody. Our experience is a mental construct originating from the vibrational frequencies of our thoughts, which in turn power up our feelings and emotions.

Thoughts are the seeds we plant in the creative soil of our minds until they take root and grow into the beliefs and values which underpin our decisions. When we plant disempowering, fear-based thoughts and embody them in our emotions, beliefs, values and actions, they'll grow into undesirable circumstances and unhealthy conditions around us.

Likewise, when we plant empowering, useful seeds—harmony, goodness and success will grow around us. The adage of we reap what we sow, is true. Our life is not random. Our life is what we make it by the resonance of our Consciousness because all form is first thought, repeated, embodied, enacted and energized.

Individual thoughts form patterns of thought which

become our mindset which influence our everyday experiences and reality. Whether we want to accept the fact or not, we *are* the masters of our destiny, for when we make our mind up, we run into the evidence of it.

Scientific and psychological observations reveal important discoveries of how the mind works. Firstly, the mind can't distinguish between the real and the imaginary. Whether we're watching a scene from a movie or a scene in real life, our mind doesn't make distinctions. This explains why some actors have difficulty after playing horrific on-screen characters. Their mind is overwhelmed by the apparent acts of violence and emotions which until then weren't part of their frame of reference. The performance is so real and heightened by high levels of energy, that the actor's state of mind or mindset is radically changed. It may take some time and conscious therapy to restore equilibrium or in some cases, the actor reverts to drugs or suicide to deal with their panicked state of being.

Our mind digests ideas much like our body digests food. If we feed our minds trash, we create a future wasteland. Therefore, what is our mental diet? What are we watching, reading, listening to and talking about? Is it fear or faith-based? Because whatever it is, it's having an enormous impact on our lives. More importantly, what is our children's mental diet? What are they watching, reading, listening to and talking about? If we feed our children's minds trash, we create more than a future wasteland, we create generations of toxic waste.

This time is challenging enough for young minds as they try to understand what has happened to the world they knew, without being fed a diet of fear. As adults, we must be extra loving and vigilant that we're feeding our children's mind the best food we can, so they have the nutrients to develop a Master Mindset. The world's going to need a lot of Mindset Masters when this is all over.

Ninety-five percent of our mind's activity comes from the subconscious, which like a gigantic computer, has stored everything that has ever happened to us. We're bombarded with two million bits of data every second and it's the job of the subconscious to filter through this. The conscious mind remembers between five and nine pieces of information which is then passed onto the subconscious to free up conscious space for processing. Since we live most of our lives on automatic pilot, we must become more conscious if we want to live happier, healthier and wealthier lives. According to Carl Jung, "Until you make the unconscious conscious, it will direct your life, and you will call it fate."

Everything we've ever been exposed to and then interpreted, learned and applied through our thoughts, perceptions, beliefs, values, emotions, words, actions and memories has left an imprint on our unconscious mind. These are not dead things. They are always active, impacting our Consciousness.

Therefore, we must stand at the gateway to our thoughts, perceptions and beliefs, and only allow those that identify love and faith entry into the fertile soil of our minds and those of our children. If we want a better future, we must live a better today, resonate at the purest frequency we can and permit only empowering mind food to feed our mental facet.

Mental inactivity, limitation and lack lead to poor mental health, which in turn produces poor results, energetically and in our reality. Unfortunately, many people choose mental laziness. They become complacent in their reasoning, slothful of thought, and they scorn wisdom. Instead of expanding their intelligence, they settle for what they have, rather than what they're capable of. Each of us has free-will choice not to be influenced by the fear-based messages presented by the media, social platforms, education, political, religious and societal systems, yet many people allow this negativity to shape their lives. In doing so, they become anxious, depressed and even bitter toward those who have more, do more, or are *being* more. A sinister sense of resentment and entitlement pervades their consciousness as they settle for less, expecting others to make up for the shortfall in their lives. But when we function from a Master Mindset, we know we're responsible for our mental health.

There are several activities that can assist in developing and strengthening a healthy mindset. Firstly, embark on a self-development campaign during this time. Just like this book, there are numerous resources and online courses available. Make the investment to fast-track your life. You may say you can't afford it, but can you really afford not to? Watch inspirational movies, read empowering books, listen to inspiring podcasts, book into an online course and participate in positive conversations that promote a purer frequency of

Consciousness. As previously mentioned, exercise and diet have also been shown to positively influence mindset, so use this time to reevaluate these areas of your life, set new goals and get started.

Most of us know that a cluttered environment contributes to a cluttered mind. Isolation is a terrific time to spring clean the house, toss out what doesn't serve you any longer and do the same with your thought patterns. The outer reflects the inner, so get your mind and environment in order.

Any activity that involves concentration strengthens your mindset—mindfulness, meditation, yoga, creative projects and any practice that's executed with intensity and passion are all powerful tools in shifting from a limited, human perspective to a Master Mindset.

By combining the above activities, you'll resonate at a purer frequency of Consciousness from where you can more easily master your life.

As the great poet Rumi wrote, "The universe is not outside you. Look inside yourself. Everything that you want, you already are."

Despite what the world tells you, you stand at the threshold of limitless opportunity when you have the right mindset.

EXERCISE:

Comfort leads to complacency which is just a breath away from calamity.

Understand that if we're dead in the head, it'll only take a while for our body to follow. Therefore, to shift and strengthen our mindset, we must stretch it.

What are three activities you can commence in the next twenty-four hours that will stretch your current mindset? You may find you're already doing one or two as part of the other energetic initiatives you've implemented.

For example:

Purchase a new non-fiction book and when I read it, take notes.

List them below.

_____
_____
_____
_____
_____
_____
_____
_____

Another powerful technique is to do something you've been avoiding; like cleaning out your closet, tidying up your desk, organizing a filing system in your computer, giving your garden or pot plants some tender loving care.

Any task that you've been repeatedly putting off —do it!

Immerse yourself in it with good cheer, determination, discipline, drive and energy until it's finished. Aside from the great sense of fulfillment you'll experience on finally completing this task, you'll have unlocked another level of energy in your Consciousness.

No matter how bright or large the reality you wrote down at the end of Chapter Three, imagine it even bigger. Enlarge your thoughts and expand your Consciousness for energy fills all space and brings it into form.

Though life is inexhaustible, it's up to each of us to imagine the boundless possibilities on offer. Day by day, when we dare to *be more*, we access more of those possibilities. And soon what we originally thought of as impossibilities, become probabilities until they eventually become the actuality of our life.

**There's no scarcity of opportunity to make a living at what you love.
There is only a scarcity of resolve to make it happen.**

Dr Wayne W. Dyer

TEN

Financial Facet

Volumes have been written on how to make money, get rich quick or win big. However, the basic advice is still the best. When it comes to money, use common sense—

- Spend less than you earn
- Invest a little each week so your money multiplies
- Guard your money from loss
- Make your home a profitable investment
- Increase your ability to earn
- Give to those less fortunate
- Work by the principle of giving a fair day's work for a fair day's pay
- Ensure a future income
- And be grateful for what you have.

If you find yourself currently suffering from financial scarcity, it's because you haven't lived by the above financial principles. The ego will latch onto the biggest, most obvious principle and make excuses as to why it hasn't been possible to make your home a profitable investment. Hell, you can barely afford to pay the rent.

But what about the small things? Couldn't you have invested a little each week, so your money multiplied? Forfeited some small luxury, like a coffee or a dinner out, and popped the money aside to build a nest egg?

Everyone can. But few do. It's those few who currently find themselves in a more secure financial position during the pandemic. As George Clason wrote in *The Richest Man of Babylon*, "Better a little caution than great regret."

Still, there's a deeper Truth at work here. *Everything is energy.* If we want more money, financial security, abundance and success, we must shift our mindset with regards to substance and supply and resonate at a purer frequency of Consciousness.

Those who proclaim their disinterest and dislike of money are usually poor. It's the ego's way of excusing their beliefs of lack and limitation by criticizing that which they desire most but inherently feel they don't deserve.

However, money isn't the root of all evil. Poverty consciousness is. If we desire more money, we must disregard the ego, expand our Consciousness and *be* the embodiment which draws in the money. Our financial freedom manifests in direct proportion to our Consciousness because *we* are the source.

Everyone experiences exactly the amount of success and abundance they can justify receiving. Whether we live with prosperity or poverty consciousness, the law of attraction still applies. Whatever philosophy, values, beliefs, perceptions, thoughts, feelings, emotions and decisions we embody and energize, will return to us, like for like. Sending out the desire for more money to pay the bills, when all we think about is how much money we don't have, is nothing but wishful thinking.

Worrying over, talking about and acting out how much we don't have or why we can't afford something, only ingrains poverty consciousness in ourselves and our family.

Consider the language you use in your home regarding money. Is it one of fear and lack or one of faith and abundance? Remember, we must match the frequency of the reality we want **first**, and we cannot help but get that reality. This can seem an insurmountable task and downright stupid when there's no money in the bank to pay the bills because you've lost your job, or your business is going under. But if you want a changed reality, you must change your mindset and elevate your energy right in the midst of the turmoil. Keep reaffirming abundance and look for the opportunities and changed circumstances that will appear unexpectedly so you can make your payments. Become a money magnet because no matter how much you pursue money; it will always outrun you.

The same applies if we work only for money. Even if we're paid handsomely, if we don't derive any enjoyment or fulfillment from our wealth, we're trapped in poverty consciousness. We'll never have enough money; we'll never find time to enjoy money and no amount of money will ever be able to compensate for the lack we feel in our lives.

It's up to us to make our lives successful and fulfilling. No one else; most certainly, there's no such thing as dumb luck. Yet many people believe they're unlucky. They feel separate from their lives, believing they're powerless, and that while success and fulfillment bless others, they're left to struggle. These limiting beliefs and dense energetic resonances leave people feeling resentful. They accuse, criticize and blame successful people as if they're somehow responsible for their lowly lot. Suffering from a deep-rooted sense of inequality, they fail to understand we're all equal. We're all one Consciousness in expression.

When we realize we're not dealing with the form of money and success, but with the *energy* of abundance and supply, we graduate into an enhanced resonance of prosperity consciousness. Instead of seeing our financial freedom outside of ourselves, we shift to seeing ourselves as the source of our supply, of our abundance. The more we expand our Consciousness, the more abundance multiplies in our lives. And until we're willing to *be* of value and of service to others, very little of value will manifest in our lives.

If we're expanding our Consciousness, aligning ourselves to our *being* and supporting it with action, we're living in the space of prosperity consciousness. Because we're adding value and *being* more, we're attracting more success into our lives. This success manifests in different forms, as people, opportunities, money, a new job or contract, or a loving relationship.

Conversely, if our habits focus on lack and limitation, we're dwelling in the space of poverty consciousness, and we'll reap reciprocal results.

Once we know that our *being* is the source of our supply and abundance, we need only align ourselves with it and move forward. Abundance and supply always respond when the desire and dreams that we dare to fling into Consciousness, reflect the fulfillment of our *being*.

There is law, order, harmony and an infinite intelligence to the universe—the same intelligence which constitutes our *being*. Try as we might to ignore this infinite intelligence, we can no more change or manipulate it than we can change the rotation of the earth. As such, the power that flows through infinite intelligence flows through us, demonstrating in our reality. Because our wealth never far exceeds our Consciousness, once we align ourselves with this power and accept our inseparable connection to it, our results will reflect our blossoming prosperity consciousness. When we dare to embrace ourselves as indivisible from our success and fulfillment, we make it so.

EXERCISE:

Under each of the below statements, write down your first, spontaneous response. Don't censor it in any way.

Avalanches of abundance rain down on me in all areas of my life.

_____
_____
_____
_____

Making money for me is easy because I have the Midas touch.

_____
_____
_____
_____

I give thanks that the millions of dollars which are mine, now pour in and pile up in perfect ways.

_____
_____
_____
_____

I give wonderful service for wonderful pay.

_____
_____
_____
_____

I give thanks for my continuing, ongoing and unbridled success.

_____
_____
_____
_____

Your answers will demonstrate which consciousness - prosperity or poverty - you function from, as do the results in your life. Every time you think, speak or act lack and limitation around money, catch yourself, become more conscious and use these five affirmations to shift your mindset to a prosperity consciousness.

Being **is neither behind the point of perfection or advancing towards it.**
It is at the point and must be understood there from.

Mary Baker Eddy

ELEVEN

Spiritual Facet

Because we are one Consciousness, uniquely and individually expressed in human form, none of us amount to anything on your own. Since we don't exist on our own, we can't account for ourselves on our own. It's like accounting for where our lap goes when we stand up. It exists but not in its previously perceived form. We exist as conscious *being*, except we've been conditioned to perceive ourselves as human form. But that doesn't change the fact that we are all energy—Consciousness with a body.

It's obvious that what's happening in the world right now isn't going to unfold to our preconceptions. Try as we might to forecast and predict how this pandemic will play out, no one knows. The ongoing inference that there's something happening outside of ourselves that requires all our attention keeps us separated from the Truth. For there is nothing going on here but Consciousness. Once we internalize this quantum shift, our world changes, for we experience it from *being*.

Being is an experience of feeling. You cannot think yourself into manifesting a new reality, you must be willing and curious enough to feel your *being* and yield to its movement. Yet we've been conditioned to control everything—our weight, our children, our partners, our job, our time. We're control freaks. It's the ego's ultimate weapon in personal defense, because while we're defended against our world, the illusion of separateness persists.

When we're seemingly out of control and dealing with the unknown is when we have the greatest opportunity for the emergence of a new frame of reference. We become more conscious of our inner resources as we search for meaning. Our senses become more acute and refined. We experience subtle energy adjustments and if we're willing to pay attention, we feel a lightness in our body. Our Consciousness is vibrating at a purer resonance. Though we're in the world, we're not of it. That's not to say we walk around as if in a dopey daze. On the contrary, more aware and attuned, we see things we never saw before, experience things we never experienced. We are more conscious of being Consciousness in expression.

This shift happens when we withdraw our commitment to the ego and give it to the conscious experience of *being*. Sometimes, it can be accompanied by sensations of uneasiness, anxiety and tension, but instead of succumbing to these frequencies of fear and dramatizing them, we must keep the faith, lean into the experience and know that enlightenment is happening. Our *being* is pressing against our old distorted perspective and limited concepts, and in doing so, we're evolving our Consciousness so it can expand and burst forth. Being conscious doesn't destroy the world around us. It destroys the process of the ego, our limited human perspective.

That which lies beyond our sense of limitation isn't beyond our capacity to understand and comprehend. We must each dare to step beyond our limited, human perspective, in order to experience a new frame of reference, so we can master our lives.

Just like the space between the bars of a cell signify freedom to the prisoner, so does space in our lives. No matter how distracting the external world appears, no matter how many bars of busyness seem to imprison us, we must choose for space so we can be free from our conditioned thinking and limitations.

Whether it's physical as in overpopulated spaces, or mental as in the negative thoughts swimming through our minds, or emotional as in the topsy-turvy states of fear-based emotions, we lack the spiritual space to *be*. While we jam, cram and slam more stuff into our lives, we sacrifice our space, our peace and our *being*.

Currently, there's a rising desperation for the busyness in life to return rather than a willingness to *be*. But don't allow the ego traction by trying to keep you busy. Claim your space and find your peace. Not that you need a physical space, for it lies within us, and we access it through meditation. Every time we shift our attention from the bars of busyness to the space of solitude within, we align with the unfoldment of our *being*.

Our *being* is constantly calling into play our capacity to recognize this Truth.

Our *being* is constantly daring us to be the fullest expression of Consciousness.

Our *being* is constantly affirming to us that love is real, while fear is not.

Shifting from a finite to the infinite viewpoint means shifting from separateness to unity, from judgement to discernment. While we sit in judgement of ourselves, each other and the apparent events going on around us, there's little space in our lives for love. Love cannot reside where there's no space for peace.

Like the latest must-have technology, judgement has been sold to us as a global solution. In fact, we feel justified to judge. We're insidiously encouraged to rate and judge what other people wear, what they do, what they say, how they look, what gender they are, what color their skin is, what age they are and what religion they worship. Banning the labels of black, white, rich, poor, man, woman, Christian or Muslim does little to remove the judgement which is the root cause, not of the words or labels, but of the separateness of which the ego has falsely convinced us. Acts of bullying, brutality, violence and global conflict are a result of judgement, of people feeling less than or more than another, which in some cases, appear to be escalating because of the pandemic.

Judgement spreads like suffocating algae over our hearts, leaving no space for love. If we don't take responsibility for our own reality, it will extinguish love from our lives. Judgement removes kindness, patience, respect, compassion, tenderness and inclusiveness, and replaces them with resentment, contempt, hostility, intolerance, superiority and exile. When we judge, we separate ourselves from our Consciousness, from our oneness, from our unity. Ultimately, we destroy ourselves and our relationships. Know that every time we judge ourselves or another, that judgement acts like a silent sniper and will take us down. We can never master our lives or our destiny while we sit in judgement.

Being, on the other hand, is the space of peace and the expression of love. It unifies and illuminates the Truth. We must each follow the inner path of our evolving *being* as it unfolds and reveals itself as our conscious experience. This is where our integrity lies.

In simple terms, when we resonate at the purest resonant frequency emotionally, physically, mentally, financially and spiritually we align with *being*. We gain sparkling clarity and integrity and transcend the distorted experience of separateness. We become whole; our integrity is fortified. There's no need to waste time trying to intellectualize it or suffering any longer. Just go within, energize and align!

EXERCISE:

During isolation, commit to not busying yourself. Throughout the day, stop for three ten-minute breaks and retreat. This is your time for introspection and reflection. Take your notebook and pen and find a comfortable spot where you won't be disturbed. During this time, jot down one question that you'd like answered. Ask it aloud only once, then relax. If distracting thoughts surface, that's just the ego scrambling trying to keep you busy while your *being* is calling you to peace, stillness, introspection and reflection. Redirect your mind to your question and write down any ideas or thoughts that come to you. Don't think them through or judge them. Continue being in the peace for the full ten minutes before finishing with gratitude.

Over the coming days and week, repeat this exercise, reviewing the answers from sessions and actively searching for the pattern of solutions and suggestions. They'll be there but it won't be your intellect that will deliver them to you. They'll come from going within to *being*.

_____
_____
_____
_____
_____
_____
_____

The secret to change is to focus all of your energy, not on fighting the old, but on building the new.

Socrates

TWELVE

Future Focus

Where your focus goes, energy flows and results will surely follow. If we want to change the results in our life, it's our responsibility to *consistently* focus on the future reality we desire most. We must resonate at the purest frequency of our Consciousness and enact, embody and energize that future every moment we can through our values and beliefs, perceptions, thoughts, feelings, decisions, actions and habits. When considered from this perspective, it's simple. So why do we find it so difficult? Because we lack the focus to stay the course and the energy to get it done. We just give up.

According to research, human attention span has markedly decreased. In 2000, it was twelve seconds but in 2015, it shrank significantly to just over eight seconds. In fact, scientists estimate we now have shorter attention spans than goldfish, who're able to focus on a task or object for nine seconds. This explains why only eight percent of the people who set goals, actually manifest them.

The ego has hooked us into a limited human perspective where we're easily distracted. Like addicts who can't get enough, we're always looking for the next high, the next big thing to stimulate us or the next obsession we just can't live without. Phones, food, clothes, movies, video games, lotteries and the list of things that pulls our focus goes on, while the destiny we desire most remains at arm's length. Our attention chops from one thing to another and back again. We rarely focus long enough to read more than a few paragraphs or pages of a book, magazine or report. That's why in the Helpful Hints to Enhance Your Experience at the beginning of this book, the list clearly explains what to do before commencing to read. Those hints serve to empower your focus.

For those people who've developed a future focus, the destiny they've always wanted is assured. Like Nelson Mandela who served twenty-eight years in prison for conspiring to overthrow the state following the Rivonia Trial. In his personal sacrifice of freedom for the greater good, his focus never wavered from his mission for a peaceful and more equal society in South Africa. On the day of his release, he said, "As I walked out the door toward the gate that would lead to my freedom, I knew if I didn't leave my bitterness and hatred behind, I'd still be in prison." He released everything that didn't serve him and kept his focus firmly on his mission and the reality he wanted. And it manifested. This is the power of steadfast focus.

In physics, the impact of focus was discovered in the double split experiment to observe the behavior of subatomic particles. The experiment reveals that the act of observation itself influences how particles behave. Think about that. The act of someone observing the particle can impact how it behaves. Unless tests are conducted as a double-blind, meaning the technician doesn't know what they're looking for, the results aren't definitive because the technician's act of observation can influence the results. Imagine the impact we have on our lives and those around us purely by the act of observation. That's why watching our children complete a task ensures it gets done and why focus is fundamental to changing our lives.

A future focus is vastly improved by journaling. You've been using this process at the end of the chapters throughout this book and perhaps adding more of your thoughts and ideas in your notebook along the way. The more you review, refine and repeat the process the stronger and more laser-focused your mindset becomes. That's why journaling your vision, intention, goals and action strategies is necessary to energizing and attracting your future into your present. Just keeping the ideas in your mind isn't enough. They'll get lost with all the other data floating around in there. But when you commit them to paper, they provide a blueprint from which to build your new life. The same applies for vision boards that give a visual representation of how you want your new life to be. Any form of recording helps to shape the reality you desire most. And the more of the five senses you engage in the process, the more you'll match the frequency of the reality you want.

Throughout life, most of us focus our attention on

our personality. We're obsessed with doing things to give meaning to our personality—doing a job, doing the chores, doing the family commitments, and the to-do list gets longer. We do our lives in order to have things— have a better job, have more money, have a bigger house, have more loving relationships. Our personality craves to have things, seducing us into doing more so it can have more. *Doing* and *having* cannibalize our time, peace and sanity. This addiction to doing and having is endemic in Western civilization, as evidenced by chronic levels of stress, fear and depression.

Now with the added applied pressure because of the pandemic, many people have lost the activities they enjoyed and the things that gave them significance. This shock has further compounded their conflicted state of being because they can no longer *do* and *have* as before. They've been cast adrift from the life they knew. A new rudder is needed.

Time to reconnect with and focus on *being*. For despite everything we've been conditioned to believe, an abundant, loving, successful and healthy life is *not* about doing and having. It's about *Being*. When we shift our focus away from our puny personality to *being*, the doing and the having are no longer distorted by the energy of ego-centric achievement, but naturally unfold in perfect alignment in an energy of elegance. The coronavirus is a major lesson teaching us that life isn't about what we have or what we do. It's about who we're *being*, as individuals, in relationships, in families and in communities. Who we're *being* during this time sets the benchmark for our health, wealth and happiness at the other end of the pandemic.

EXERCISE:

We create chaos because we focus on chaotic circumstances and conditions. We judge ourselves and others harshly, instead of focusing on our Consciousness, our *being*, which identifies everyone and everything as one. Life's challenges aren't meant to paralyze us. They're supposed to help us uncover our *being*.

List the top ten things you focussed on before the pandemic and describe them.

For example:
I had a job that paid the bills, but I complained a lot about how I didn't like it.
I wanted to take the kids out more but made excuses because I was too tired.

_____
_____
_____
_____
_____
_____
_____
_____
_____
_____
_____
_____
_____
_____
_____

Next to each one, write whether they applied to the being, doing or having aspects of your life.
Now write the ten top things you're going to focus on *being*, starting from today.

_____
_____
_____
_____
_____
_____
_____
_____
_____
_____
_____
_____
_____
_____
_____
_____
_____
_____
_____
_____
_____
_____

We are all living in paradise. It's time to stop focussing on hell.

Rather than asking for more—which implies shortages and, therefore, creates a vibrational match to more shortages—focus on what you have and how thankful you are for everything that has shown up in your life.

Dr Wayne W. Dyer

THIRTEEN

Gratitude or Grief

In her 1969 book *On Death and Dying*, Elisabeth Kübler-Ross first proposed that there were the five stages of grief—denial, anger, bargaining, depression and acceptance.

These stages of grief are universal and experienced by people across the world, regardless of culture, status or race. Different events trigger the grief response including an individual's own terminal illness, the loss of a close relationship either personal or professional, or the death of a loved one or animal, and as the pandemic is demonstrating, the loss of pre-coronavirus life.

During the grief process, we spend various amounts of time working through each stage and express each with different intensities of energy. Though we may experience the stages in any order, the aim is to move through into peaceful acceptance. Some people may openly express their emotions; some may suppress them, some may channel the energy into physical or creative pursuits, while some may transmute the energy with love and forgiveness. Others are inspired to reevaluate their own lives during the process, to make new decisions and shift their mindset. Everyone is different, but in the end a common thread emerges—hope. If one has hope, there is always life.

Many countries and communities are expounding the message of hope as their citizens hibernate in forced isolation at this time. Though it's worth noting that isolation is associated with denial in the grief process. Shutting oneself away can lead to further grieving if not managed properly. Though concerns of governments for the loss of life during the pandemic is commendable, perhaps more consideration needs to be given to the anger brewing and depression seeping into the minds of millions of people. Unfortunately, this may have more far-reaching, long-term generational effects than the short-term accumulative deaths. Since everything is energy, the horror of the death experience isn't real. It's another distortion of our limited perspective. For how could we die if we're Consciousness forever creating and individualizing itself? We just change form.

However, the death of a loved one is one of the most confronting events of this truth, especially during this time when a last touch or kiss isn't allowed. For those of us left behind, the sense of separation can feel both intimately real and intellectually surreal. The sense of loss can be acute and for some, chronic.

But isn't it the loss of the familiar which is really the issue as we begin a new life, seemingly alone and separated from the one we loved? It's in this state of misplaced separateness that we're likely to give our ego carte blanche to regurgitate every fear-based emotion. Heartache, grief, self-doubt, guilt, indecision, blame, worthlessness, anger, inadequacy, fear of the future—an endless litany of emotions creeps up like silent raiders in the night to distract us from the truth.

It's important though not to stop the expression of this emotional energy for any energy blocked at its initial expressive need leads to disease at some later stage. However, in the expression of our grief, we have the opportunity to express gratitude, knowing that as conscious *being*, we're in no way affected by death. Just because we can't physically see, hear, smell, taste or touch the one who has died, doesn't mean they don't exist as Consciousness. And since we're all the activity of Consciousness in expression, we're all one. We're of the one source, the one Consciousness which is eternally creating and moving, and never dies.

The energy of gratitude is one of the most powerful liberators of the grief process. It fixes our focus on being optimistic rather than pessimistic, on hope rather than despair. We begin to view life as a glass half full, rather than half empty, until we realize that our glass isn't just half full, it's overflowing.

Studies have shown that when a person is grateful, specific parts in the brain associated with memory light up. The connections in the brain become stronger, and we seek out similar feel-good experiences. The more grateful we are, the more we have to be grateful for. The more we light up our brain with gratitude, the more we light up those around us with our energy. Gratitude helps us shine a light on what's right in the world rather than what's wrong. It's resonance illuminates our lives and acts as a beacon for the reality we desire most to find us.

Conscious active gratitude is the practice of being thankful in a mindful, energized manner. On first waking in the morning give thanks for the day ahead, expecting it to deliver magic and miracles to you. Then throughout the day, be aware of the gifts life brings and give thanks for them. No matter how small, be grateful. When you go to bed at night, give thanks for your perfect day and the deep, restorative sleep you're going to receive. Sleeping tablets are never needed when we practice conscious active gratitude.

Even when there appears nothing to be grateful for, it is up to each of us to find it. Like a children's game, we must hunt out the precious treasures that hide in our life and appreciate them. Be they things, people, activities or pets, we must stop and say thank you. We can even appreciate the coronavirus for its immediate effect on the planet in bringing people together with more compassion. All it takes is a shift of perspective.

The more we practice conscious active gratitude, the more our worldview changes and subsequently our own personal reality changes. When we live with gratitude we glorify our Consciousness and attract to ourselves more to be thankful for.

EXERCISE:

Gratitude is a force for good—an energetic resonance that signals our mind to expect more. Its resonance and radiance act as a vibrational magnet which gives birth to fulfilment and success.

List ten aspects of your life that you're thankful for.

_____
_____
_____
_____
_____
_____
_____
_____
_____
_____
_____

List at least two ways that you can include conscious active gratitude each day in your life.

_____
_____
_____
_____
_____
_____
_____

Another powerful exercise to include in your routine is as a family. During the evening meal, everyone shares what they are grateful for that day. It must be something considered, thoughtful and different each day. It sets a loving tone for the evening meal while encouraging children to appreciate the blessings in life. Keep a family journal of these blessings and how they influence the family dynamic. You may be surprised by the transformational power of conscious active gratitude.

**We need silence
to be able to touch our souls.**

Mother Theresa

FOURTEEN

Meditation – Our Natural State of Being

Each of us is a living, resonating field of energy directly impacting our reality. Because of the advances in technology, we can now monitor and correlate how a change of Consciousness affects physical reality. In simple terms, change our mindset, change our Consciousness, change our reality. And regular meditation is the most powerful tool to fast track this change because it sidesteps our intellect and rational thinking.

Contrary to popular belief, meditation isn't an altered state of mind. The ego is the altered state of mind. The limited human perspective is a distorted viewpoint and when we live from this fear-based perspective, we can be nothing but reactive to ourselves, others and the world. Meditation is the experience of *being* infinite, intelligent mind and goes deeper than a few minutes of mindfulness. It's the direct experience of Consciousness in expression, which is sometimes referred to as bliss Consciousness, for it is truly heavenly.

If you're a novice at meditation the first step is to

enjoy solitude because it's impossible to find happiness without solitude. The pandemic we find ourselves in is like a gift from heaven because isolation is the best opportunity you'll ever get to begin your meditation practice. As you learn to shift your attention from the external to the internal world, you'll come to appreciate that you're in good company. For the wisdom gained from going within will never lead you astray and will sustain you more than anyone or anything else in your life.

In the silence is where we ignore our thoughts and lose our misguided belief of separateness. When we become still and settle into the depths of ourselves as Consciousness, we escape from the limited human perspective by withdrawing our attention from the ego and giving it within to *being*. Meditation is the ultimate demonstration of love for ourselves. A time to go within to the peace at the center of our *being*, experience our all-oneness and focus on the light, energetically and visually.

There are four states to meditation; being centered, being curious, being receptive and being in communion. Being centered involves stillness and focus with our attention on nothing but the center of our *being*. This alignment with *being* can be enhanced by a variety of practices including breathing techniques, visualizations and guided meditations, but must be accompanied by absolute willingness and infinite patience. No matter how long being centered takes, we must be willing and patient enough to dwell in this space before continuing. Without being centered, our mind will simply reboot, and thoughts will tumble forth unabated. A simple visualization to practice is to still our mind until it becomes like the surface of a deep, languid lake on a still day, gently moving without effort or resistance. Thoughts may come and go, but our role is to disregard them. Persist with being centered even if feels like it never happens. On a deep level, we're making radical change and we must trust that this is so.

It's like Aesop's fable of the cheeky hare challenging the tortoise to a race. The hare is the obvious choice to win because of his speed and agility, while the tortoise is too cumbersome. But in the end, the tortoise wins. The moral of the story was slow and steady wins the race. The same applies to meditation. There's no rush to get there, slow and steady wins out in the end. Just keep going within.

Once centered, the next step is to be curious. Like a child sitting on the edge of the lake gazing out across the water into the distance not looking for anything in particular, we must continue searching to see if anything of interest is there. This is the casual, yet concentrated curiosity needed.

Being curious opens the way to being receptive, of listening, of being open and aware. The more we meditate the more well detach from third-dimensional reality and discern the movement of Consciousness. We might experience this movement through what's known as the four 'Clairs' which relate to enhanced sensory perception beyond our normal five senses. Clairvoyance means clear seeing, where we receive images in our mind. The images may hold special significance to us and when we see them, their meaning is clear. Clairaudience relates to hearing messages from what is often referred to as the still, small voice within. More often than not, this voice may sound like our own with a softer more loving tone. Nevertheless, the guidance given is always compassionate, never critical. Claircognizance is receiving a clear knowing that cannot be denied. We just know things. We don't know how we know them; we just do. The last is clairsentience which means clear feeling where we receive messages as feelings.

In each of the four 'Clairs', it's the experience that matters. Though it's difficult to adequately explain, most people have experienced it as a gut instinct or intuition. Its message appears as if from nowhere, but you know you didn't make it up in your head. This self-knowing originated in your solar plexus region, from your gut. And if you follow its advice, it's always correct.

The ego's voice of ridicule will try to insinuate we're crazy, but we must ignore it and hold firm to being centered, curious and receptive. For once we master these steps, our normal day-to-day experience lifts from us, allowing our *being* to be consciously experienced which leads us into the experience of communion.

Being in communion with everything and knowing everything is Consciousness eternally expressing itself, brings absolute peace. A peace of mind which renders poise and aligns us with *being*. Doubt, uncertainty and anxiety are gone.

During the pandemic, meditation is a godsend. For instead of believing everything we see and hear, we can go within, ask a question and expect an answer. It can be as simple as asking what's the most appropriate action to take in any current circumstance. We ask it once, then remain centered, curious and open to receive the answer from our inner guidance. When we receive a message, our responsibility is to act on it. Practical and meaningful, the practice of meditation attunes us to realms of expanded awareness, health and energy beyond what we've been conditioned to expect.

We've spent too much time giving our inherent intelligence and power away to other authorities. Like gullible lemmings, we've been following each other off the cliffs of Consciousness and drowning in our fears for too long. Time to stop. Go within and refer to the wisest authority of all—*Being*.

The greatest benefit from meditation comes from regular practice. As the saying goes, practice makes perfect and the daily experience of our peace sustains us in troubled times. As our connection to our peace becomes stronger, we build more faith and trust in ourselves. The daily practice of meditation keeps fresh this peace experience and provides us with a choice to activate this energy whenever necessary. Meditation helps us to engage with our inner resources and deal with our life with dignity and elegance.

EXERCISE:

The excuse most people use not to meditate is that they don't have the time. Yet they have time to watch television, play on their phones, fluff around on Facebook, trawl Twitter and do other mindless activities. The real reason why people don't meditate is that they lack resolve. They can't be bothered because they can't see demonstrable results straight away. Their ego is looking for the next quick fix to keep them locked in a limited human perspective while meditation is the key to escape their entrapment for good.

Where do you sit on the sliding scale of regular daily meditation? How often do you meditate, if at all?

_____
_____
_____
_____

What excuses do you use not to meditate?

_____
_____
_____
_____

Do those excuses make your life better?

_____
_____
_____
_____

Exercise 14

Do those excuses give you more peace?

_____
_____
_____
_____

How can you overcome those excuses?

_____
_____
_____
_____

The key with meditation is to ritualize it by making a small sacred space in your home where you'll meditate every day, even if it's for just fifteen minutes. What's important is that you meditate regularly and preferably at the same time as this signals to your mind and body your expectation for peaceful quiet. Set up a small table or corner somewhere in your home, and dress it with candles, incense, crystals or photos. Include whatever *feels* right for you. Select meditation music that inspires you to go within, and ensure you find a comfortable position. One where your breathing is unobstructed, and your muscles are relaxed, so your body doesn't hold tension. Then be still and centered, be curious, be receptive and be in communion.

Over time, taking these minutes for yourself won't fill you with uneasiness or guilt. The world will go on without you. And you'll come to appreciate that meditation is not only the best gift you can give yourself but also your family. For what greater way to bring peace to your home life than if the entire family learns to meditate.

As the Dalai Lama said, "If every eight-year-old in the world is taught meditation, we will eliminate violence from the world within one generation."

Meditation Checklist:

1. Set up a sacred space
2. Decorate it with candles, incenses, crystals, photos or other meaningful items
3. Eliminate all distractions
4. Select meditation music or guided visualizations you enjoy
5. Ensure comfortable seating where you can remain still for at least twenty minutes without fidgeting or getting 'pins-and-needles.'
6. Begin with cyclical breathing and focus.

Your children are not your children.
They are the sons and daughters of Life's
longing for itself.
They come through you but not from you and
though they are with you,
yet they belong not to you.

Khalil Gibran

FIFTEEN

Parenting as the Presence of Peace

One of the catch-cries of children is that they're bored. More rightly, their egos lack stimulation, excitement and control. Like us, children suffer from poverty consciousness, a lack mentality about themselves and their lives. And because they've even less control in their lives because of their status in the family unit, their egos rebel every chance they get.

But the truth is, children are Consciousness expressing itself in every moment, the same as adults. If the purest resonant frequency of Consciousness isn't being demonstrated by the child because of a mentality of lack and limitation, it doesn't mean that Consciousness doesn't exist. It doesn't mean that child is unlovable. It's just that the child's energetic field is distorted by the energy of the ego. And like us, the child feels anxious on the inside, but unless he or she has been taught how to deal with these emotions, they mirror the behavior of their ego-centric parents. And war ensues.

If as parents and carers we registered the Truth

about our children, that they're no less than us, that they are Consciousness that is, that has been and always will be, our approach to them would vastly change as would our children's behavior. While we try to control, manipulate, struggle with and finally succumb to their egos, we're in a losing battle because kids have a vast reservoir of hormones raging through their bodies they can access for added energy. Their recent incarnation has provided them with a different tool kit for this century and the memory of their past life still lies readily accessible in their subconscious. They also aren't responsible for the 'adult' things in life yet like having a job, paying bills and feeding the family. Kids' egos have got it all worked out and will challenge their parents' egos every chance they can get, particularly if challenge and confrontation are the family dynamic.

That's why it's imperative for parents and carers to be the presence of peace because the ego has no defense against peace. Peace is kryptonite to the ego. During this time of isolation and social distancing, parents and children will spend more time together without the normal distractions of school, team sports, singing, dance or art classes, friends, and sleepovers. The novelty will wear off fast. Even though home schooling takes up a few hours in the day, there's lots of time left to occupy in a healthy, loving way that will bond rather than break the family unit.

It's not a parent's responsibility to keep their children's egos placated or satisfy their demands. It's their responsibility to shift the family dynamic and for parents to be the presence of peace so children can learn the important lesson of self-responsibility through loving example and not forceful manipulation.

Being in our peace doesn't render us impotent as people or parents. It unleashes our power because it eliminates our limited human perspective and gives us access to our calm, collected knowing. Peace helps us step out from our small sense of personality and observe all that is going on from a Master Mindset, from *being*. Like us, children long for peace, for connection to their *being* and they look to us as examples of how to access that deeper Truth. If we're demonstrating fear, lack and control, our children will return it to us like for like. Children are the ultimate mirror, reflecting what we need to be most aware of in our own lives. The law of attraction shines bright in our kids.

Even if we're not currently living with a Master Mindset, meditating or mastering our lives, there are still a few ways we can be the presence of peace and enrich our lives and those of our children during these times.

One of the quickest remedies to boredom is to help others. Teaching children gratitude for their blessings and how to be of service to those less fortunate instils in them life mastery habits. Start the day as a family with a gratitude meditation, prayer or conversation. It need be only a few minutes, but the energy will set the tone for the day. Then brainstorm how you can help those less fortunate in that day. Perhaps buy a couple of extra groceries and give it to the lady next door living by herself as a care package or calling older relatives more regularly. Join online groups with similar missions to serve and help. Give to a worthwhile charity such as saving animals or the forests or the oceans. Spend time together researching the various causes before making a decision, because this is the energy you want more of in your home. More of, "How can I serve? Who can I help?" Rather than "I'm bored. What about me?"

Use this time to get to really know your children rather than just entertain them. As a family, limit the time on your phones and electronic devices. Not just for the kids, but for the adults as well. Turn them off and have face-to-face discussions on the bigger issues of life —values, beliefs, money, future focus. If you approach your children from a Master Mindset expecting them to be more, they will be. Their *being* already knows the Truth, they're just waiting for you to speak and enact it. These types of deeper conversations will shift the family dynamic which in turn will change your lives and those of the generations that will follow in your family. Your influence is far-reaching. Make it intelligent, loving and peaceful.

Ban all negative language and actions in the house. Tough call, but if the energy of fear, blame and judgement is left to fester in your home, you cannot but help get that reality. You'll attract it in. Instead, encourage and reward positive language and action. Be the living example of this behavior and reap the reciprocal results.

If emotions such as anger, frustration and impatience arise, channel that energy into creative projects. This energy is a powerful force for change and if used correctly can open vast stores of previously hidden talents. Drawing, writing, experimenting, mechanics, lego, dancing, cooking, baking even knitting and crocheting are fun things to learn together, testing your dexterity and creativity. There are so many opportunities and activities to unleash children's imagination and creativity that you'll run out of time trying to complete them. The wail of "There's nothing to do," will fade into a distant past if you're prepared.

Being the presence of peace means reminding your children of who they truly are, their interconnectedness to everything because everything is energy. This can be demonstrated through developing a closeness with nature. Discuss how we separate ourselves from this one Consciousness with labels such as trees, grass, birds, flowers, dogs, cats and so on. If possible, grow a few seeds indoors and watch the awe-inspiring cycle of life. Discuss how there are seasons to life as there are in nature, and that we're going through a winter at the moment. A time to plan for Spring and plant new seeds, new thoughts in the fertile soil of our minds. Go one step further in nature and explore the unseen realms of fairies, nature spirits and elves and discover what your children think about these topics. Even if you can't get outside, there are dozens of books available online you can review together. The discussion is to energize awareness, not to convince or contradict. In the peaceful, non-judgemental space you create, you'll be surprised how much your children will reveal themselves. For younger children, they may even remember being born. And if you're fortunate to have that discussion, you'll never be the same again.

At this time, more than ever before, every family has a golden opportunity to reconnect and awaken. To explore a new way of *being* as Consciousness in expression, not as parents and children, but as universal energetic beings.

Life is a vast tapestry interwoven with limitless possibilities and realities. We each have a choice which thread to pull, which thread to weave. Your children are not with you by accident. They have chosen you. Serve them well.

EXERCISE:

Generally, families grow but not evolve. They get larger or smaller, but not evolve past a limited human perspective to a heighted awareness of a Master Mindset. Yet, whether they're aware or not, at the heart of every family lies their core values. What is most important to you? What are you willing to sacrifice for the greater good? In difficult times when a choice must be made, how would you do it? Could you do so with certainty and unanimous agreement that you're making the best choice? The answers to these and many more life-changing questions lie in the family's core values. Except most families have never discussed these or are even aware of their existence.

Now is the time to find out. Gather the family together and on the below **Family Value Hierarchy**, list every value you can think of, one to a line, in the left-hand column in no particular order. For example, love, health, contribution, fun, wisdom, family, friends, intimacy, service, wealth, freedom, education, happiness and more. Brainstorm all those aspects of life which mean a lot. If you have a bigger list, still write them all down. Everyone must have their say.

My Family Value Hierarchy

	1.
	2.
	3.
	4.
	5.
	6.
	7.
	8.
	9.
	10.
	11.
	12.
	13.
	14.
	15.
	16.
	17.
	18.
	19.
	20.

For the next part of the exercise, use a pencil and an eraser as you may end up changing this many times before you reach a unanimous decision. In the right-hand column, begin to eliminate which values are least important. For example, if adventure is the least important value to your family, you would place it next to **20.**

Then place the next least important value next to **19.** Using this process of elimination, work your way through the entire left-hand column list until you've transferred them across to the right-hand column.

This exercise may take some time and lots of debate, but it will be enlightening. Of real interest will be the top five family values you finally agree upon.

The completed **Family Value Hierarchy** can be reproduced, printed and framed as a treasured possession in your home. Its importance will be quickly realized because it's a resource everyone can reference and use as the blueprint for all future family meetings, acceptable behaviors and expected outcomes. Your **Family Value Hierarchy** will minimize arguments and maximize communication. It will be the founding principle on which your family can evolve, prepare for a brighter future and launch into the new world which awaits you.

Creativity doesn't wait for that perfect moment. It fashions its own perfect moments out of ordinary ones.

Bruce Garrabrandt

SIXTEEN

Imagination, Creativity and Inspiration

There's a wonderful story which illustrates the simple yet extraordinary energy of imagination, creativity and inspiration. In 1960, the founder of Random House Publishing challenged Dr. Seuss, an acclaimed children's book author of the time to write an entertaining children's book using only fifty different words. The result was a little book called *Green Eggs and Ham* that's been a best seller since. Dr. Seuss had nothing to prove as an author, however he accepted the challenge and channeled his imagination, creativity and inspiration into the confines of fifty words. Quite a feat, but not when this energy is directed and given a willing channel.

Drew Dennis describes imagination and creativity this way, "While creativity is hard to pin down precisely, it's generally considered as the ability to create something using the imagination. Creativity is the act of creating something in the real world, while imagination deals with 'unreal' thoughts that are free from the confines of reality."

Unfortunately, too many people give up connecting with their imagination, creativity and inspiration as they get older. They mistakenly believe they're too busy with the kids, work, family and commitments to give themselves any time to play the guitar, paint, sing or engage in the creative expression or project. It's this sacrificing of the very thing which identifies our *being*, that distorts the resonant frequency of our Consciousness.

Imagination, creativity and inspiration are in a league of their own when it comes to helping us resonate at purer frequencies. They bend, blend and break the rules of third-dimensional reality to create something new or refresh what already exists in a new way, like *Green Eggs and Ham*. Whether it be the arts, literature, architecture, food, business, or fashion, no matter which aspect of life, all pursuits involve imagination and creativity. As Einstein said, "Logic will get you from A to B. Creativity will get you anywhere."

Those with a limited human perspective often believe that they're not creative and they lack imagination, but this isn't true. It's just that they haven't unlocked that energy and accessed their inner resources.

Again, this period of isolation is prime time to tap in and let the creative juices flow by either beginning that creative project you've wanted to start for ages or returning to a creative endeavor you gave up years ago. Invest this time into the energy of imagination, creativity and inspiration and have some fun.

Take the example of Isaac Newton, who back in 1665 had to work from home when the University of Cambridge temporarily closed due to the Bubonic plague. It turned out to be the most productive period of his life, because he used this time to develop his theories on calculus, optics and gravity. Though we mightn't be destined to create new scientific theory like Newton, we each impact our personal reality and by association the world at large. So, let's not waste our isolation time any longer. Let's get creative!

We begin with preparation and assimilating the basic information we're going to build on. We must decide on the project we're going to invest our time in and then try something new with it. Get off the path of least resistance, push boundaries and stretch beyond the familiar. We must dare to succeed, knowing there are no mistakes, just results we can change.

During this time, we incubate and REST. Random Episodic Silent Thought is like day dreaming where we relax and think about whatever comes to mind. Many times, we tap into rich, personal episodic memories which are a great source for creativity.

You may have experienced these moments throughout your life when you suddenly got an idea for something when you were involved in a mindless task. Writing down these ideas and thoughts straight away ensures we catch them because they're usually gone in seconds. That's why the practice of journaling helps. With your notebook and pen close at hand you don't miss a creative thought or idea. The next time you're tempted to scold your child for daydreaming, remember they're incubating and unlocking REST. They may be on the verge of a great discovery. Let them be.

The next stage in the creative process is the 'aha' or

eureka moment. This happens when all the inputs get fashioned into new ideas, and inspiration comes flooding in. These are the moments of magic and miracles, when the ordinary becomes extraordinary.

Inspiration doesn't have to be grand and world changing. It can be small and insightful. It can come to us in different ways; through movies, songs, the words of a friend, books, an idea that beams in during the twilight space between sleep and wakefulness, in meditation or while we're jogging around the park. It happens any time and usually when we least expect it. That's because we're being *inspired*, which means 'in-spirit'. It's that moment when we disconnect from the limited human perspective and yield into *being*. That's where inspiration comes from—not from our intellect or best thinking. Being inspired is proof that we're not just a body with Consciousness. That we are, indeed, Consciousness in human form.

The last stage is to put these insights and concepts together in a useful form or something that can be communicated to others. What's the point of all this delicious imagination, creativity and inspiration if we don't produce something which give us and other people value or pleasure?

Although the obvious health benefits such as relieving stress, increasing brain plasticity, transmuting emotions, enhancing mood, and anchoring positive states of being are worth it even if we don't end up producing anything.

In whatever form it takes, the creative expression of our *being* is critical to resonating to the purest frequency of our Consciousness. When we reconnect with our creative expression, we become a conduit for more joy, playfulness, hope and spontaneity to appear our lives.

Patanjali wrote, "When you are inspired by some great purpose, some extraordinary project, all your thoughts break their bonds, your mind transcends limitations, your Consciousness expands in every direction and you find yourself in a new, great and wonderful world. Dormant forces, faculties and talents come alive and you discover yourself to be a greater person by far than you ever dreamed yourself to be."

EXERCISE:

It's easier to be a critic than a creator. Who are you?

_____

Do you spend **more** of your time criticizing, rather than creating a new life, a new you, a new something that will make you happy?

_____

What creative project have you given up?

_____
_____
_____
_____

How do you creatively express yourself now?

_____
_____
_____
_____

On a scale from 1 to 5 being the highest, how much joy does this give you?_____

What would it take to make it a 5?

_____
_____
_____
_____

Exercise 16

Or is there something else you'd rather invest your energy into to express your imagination, creativity and inspiration?

_____
_____
_____
_____

What's holding you back? (Don't use the excuse of money)

_____
_____
_____

Even if you can't start that project now, what can you begin today with the intention of unlocking your imagination, creativity and inspiration? For example, cooking, baking, writing, coloring, painting, drawing, designing.

_____
_____
_____

What creative project could you begin with your children or as a family that will energize each of you to be imaginative, creative and inspired?

_____
_____
_____
_____

Begin today.

It's the repetition of affirmations that leads to belief. And once that belief becomes a deep conviction, things begin to happen.

Muhammad Ali

SEVENTEEN

Affirmations and Action

Affirmations are a powerful tool for changing thoughts, redirecting focus and resonating a purer energy. Because thought comes before form, it's reasonable to accept that affirmations can effect change in our lives. Since everything is energy, we empower the affirmations by repeatedly embodying, enacting and energizing them and in doing so, we match the frequency of the reality we want most and then get that reality.

The leading exponents in the field were Florence Scovel Shinn and Louise L. Hay and their books are veritable affirmation gold mines. They've long extolled the benefits of affirmations in shifting mindset, manifesting and understanding the mental causes for physical illness. In her best-selling book, *Heal Your Body*, Louise L. Hay's summary of cause, effect and affirmations to help in the healing process is ground-breaking. Affirmations act like the arrow with which we take aim before releasing our desire into Consciousness to hit the target. Our role is to become expert archers. For those committed to resonating at their purest energy and manifesting the reality they desire most, affirmations provide clarity and concentrated focus.

Affirmations are statements delivered with utter certainty about a perceived truth. They work because of our brain's neuroplasticity which is its ability to reorganize itself by forming new neural connections throughout life. Neuroplasticity allows the neurons (nerve cells) in the brain to compensate for injury and disease and to adjust their activities in response to new situations or to changes in their environment. Hence we can reprogram our brain through the correct use of affirmations. If our limited human perspective has programed us to get to this point in our life imagine what can be realized when we shift to a conscious Master Mindset, align with *being* and master our lives.

In fact, the Swedish furniture store IKEA conducted an experiment recently with a group of school children to demonstrate the power of intention and words on living things. As part of a social experiment, two identical house plants were placed in a controlled environment, both receiving the same amount of water and sunlight. The only variable was that one plant was exposed to a looped recording of positive affirmations, like "Seeing you blossom makes me happy". The other plant was exposed to negative phrases, such as "You look rotten." After thirty days the results were plainly visible. The plant that had been encouraged and praised was still green and lively, while the other plant that had been bullied had gone brown and began to rot. *Everything is energy.* In this experiment, the words spoken to the plants vibrated in the Consciousness and impacted the plants accordingly. The plants then matched the frequency of the words spoken and got that reality. Now consider the impact in your life of your thoughts, perceptions, beliefs, values, emotions, words, actions and habits for the past decades of your life. Like the IKEA social experiment with the plants, the results prove undeniably that you're responsible for your own reality.

To get the best out of affirmations combine all methods of learning in your practice. *Write* them out like school lessons, line after line. A sore wrist and fingers are little price to pay for a new reality. *Speak* them aloud as you stand in front of the mirror each day. Record them on your phone and *listen* to them as you go to sleep at night and first thing when you wake up in the morning. Of course, keep your phone on aeroplane mode so you won't be interrupted. Listen to them throughout the day especially when your thoughts begin to wander to stress, doubt and anxiety. Use your affirmations to improve your aim and sharpen your focus. The more you activate affirmations and integrate them into your day, the greater the power they'll unlock. Occasional use will have little impact on redirecting your focus and changing your thoughts patterns. Like meditation, daily, repeated practice will give the best results.

Always work with affirmations with specificity and in the present tense. Never design broad statements, and never place the outcome in the future. For example, you wouldn't work with a statement like, "I'm going to make a lot of money." This statement is vague, and it projects into the future, and as we know, the future never comes.

A more suitable affirmation is, "I make $100,000 this year." This is set in the present tense and states exactly how much money you make and in what timeframe. Whether this is currently true or not isn't the issue here, for the efficacy of affirmations is to suspend all disbelief when working with them. This is where the true power lies.

If you're reciting or writing an affirmation but you don't believe it, then you're wasting your time. You must place yourself into a convicted state and if that's too challenging, soften the affirmation. For example, instead of saying "I am a millionaire," which you might struggle with, change it to "Every day in every way, my financial position improves." Over time, as your position improves, you can change your affirmation until you can say with absolute conviction that you are millionaire with the expectation of witnessing that reality in the present moment.

Another clue in making affirmations work for you is to experience the truth of the statement by energizing your five senses. Visualize it, hear it, taste it, touch it, smell it—breathe in the truth of the affirmation and immerse yourself in the experience until the cells of your body tingle with the joy, success and fulfilment. Use affirmations in your meditation as a point of concentration, sending out your desire into Consciousness with absolute knowing that it will be returned to you. As Darwin P. Kingsley wrote, "You have powers you never dreamed of. You can do things you never thought you could do. There are no limitations in what you can do except the limitations of your own mind."

As your plastic, problem-solving brain responds to these new thought patterns, it will seek out how to make these affirmations a reality. When you align your brain and *being* through meditation, affirmations, conscious decision-making, responsibility and the other methods in this book, you'll match the frequency of the reality you desire most, and you will manifest it.

But you will need patience and faith. Know that you're undergoing exponential change and the ego will likely protest and try to get your attention. But remain steadfast in your inner wisdom. You've manifested your current reality so there's no reason you can't manifest a new one.

Of course, there's no point spending your precious time and energy working with affirmations if afterwards you revert to your old thoughts, actions and habits. Follow through is the name of the game now. No good affirming your wealth and deeply experiencing it in the present moment, if on receiving a bill you return to poverty consciousness and complain about there being no money. You must stop yourself, shift to prosperity consciousness, reenergize your resonance and *act as if it is already so*. Accept the bill with good cheer, being grateful that you have a roof over your head, that you have electricity, that you have food on the table. Then pay the bill knowing you are the source of your supply and abundance.

At the beginning, this shift to a Master Mindset can feel like a losing battle with the ego. But never give up. Remain committed to making your future destiny a present reality. Find solace in your solitude, affirmations and meditation. And like listening to the wise counsel of a kindly aunt, you'll receive inner guidance to help you stay the course.

Boost your new congruent decisions by taking massive consistent action in your daily activities. If you've decided to live with more faith than fear, take faith-based actions. Be more responsible, grateful, kind, conscious, elegant, loving, peaceful and creative and give up the judgement, blame, stress, anxiety and fear. Support the resonance of your enlightening Consciousness by energizing, embodying and enacting empowering actions and habits.

That's why exercise is so important. Every time you exercise and push your physical limits even if only for a small amount of time, you're grounding and recharging your body, mind and Consciousness. You're shifting your energetic field and frequency which in turn, adds energy to your day. Sometimes it's when we're exercising that we'll experience inspiration and receive our inner guidance. When we're in the 'zone' and our mind is open and receptive, we can receive the answers to the problems we've been thinking about.

Without action, we'll stagnate and die. It's not that we get old and can't move. It's that we stop moving and get old. Momentum hastens manifesting.

Affirmations are the arrows and our actions are the energy force to hit the target. With enough practice, we'll find the target easier to hit until eventually there's no distance between us and the target— the reality we desire most.

EXERCISE:

Spend some time on the internet researching affirmations. Select fifteen which you feel most drawn to, remembering they must be in the present tense, they're worded in a way that you can suspend all disbelief and that you can enthusiastically engage your five senses when working with them.

Here are a few to get you started if suitable.

1. The ground I am on is successful ground and everything good comes my way.
2. Today is my day. I live with joy, faith and hope knowing that life returns my goodness to me multiplied in wonderful ways.
3. I am the individualized expression of Consciousness in movement. The genius within me is now revealed through the perfect design of my life.
4. Today I set in motion the power of an extraordinary tomorrow.
5. I let go into the perfect order of life and am willing to embody its beauty.

6. _____

7. _____

8. _____

9. _____

10. _____

11. _____

12. _____

13. _____

14. _____

15. _____

Record them on your phone in a loop of ten minutes and play them every night and first thing in the morning when you wake up. Remember to switch your phone to aeroplane mode so as not to be disturbed.

There is nothing in the world so irresistibly contagious as laughter and good humor

Charles Dickens

EIGHTEEN

Keep it Light

Words have their own Consciousness. Like many things in our world, we take words for granted and use them unconsciously. But if we consciously examine them we often find there's a deeper meaning than what's currently applied. Take the word 'enlightenment'. The dictionary provides a straight forward definition as the action of enlightening or the state of being enlightened. If we go deeper, the word enlightened comes from the Latin prefix 'en' meaning 'in, into' and the word lux meaning 'light.' When we combine these meanings, the word describes the characteristics of an enlightened person, someone with a sense of clarity and knowing, someone who's 'in the light.'

Light also describes the frequency of energy needed to become enlightened. The lighter our energy, the more enlightened we become. Aside from the various ways already expounded in this book, there is another way to lighten our energy, through laughter and humor. Our birthright is to be happy, to feel joy bubbling up from deep within us and to share that effervescent energy with the world. We all know how good we feel when we're resonating that energy and during and after we have a good laugh. It's like all the cares of the world lift from our shoulders. We become *enlightened*.

Laughter improves our immunity by decreasing our stress hormones, increasing our immune cells and boosting infection-fighting antibodies, which is something we could all use more of now. When we're enjoying a good laugh, our brain releases its own happy drugs—endorphins—which promote an overall sense of well-being and can temporarily relieve pain. It also protects the heart and the cardio-vascular system by increasing blood flow. Though no match for exercise, laughter burns calories. Like a quick jog around the park, our insides take a little jog when we laugh. Which means a comedy is a healthier movie choice when we're lounging on the couch flicking channels. A good, belly laugh relieves tension and stress with the results being felt in our muscles for up to forty-five minutes after. And if tensions are running high in your home, nothing works better to diffuse anger and disagreement than a shared laugh. It's an intervention technique worth practicing. It's also been linked to longevity as shown by a study in Norway which indicated that those with a strong sense of humor outlived those without. That's why laughter is the best medicine.

You may recall Robin William's performance in the 1998 movie Patch Adams. A semi-biographical comedy-drama film based on the life story of Dr. Hunter "Patch" Adams who used laughter and humor as therapy much to the chagrin of his teachers. It's a poignant, funny film with its central theme encapsulated in one line from the film. "Joy is a way of life and love is the ultimate outcome."

From a social perspective we're attracted to laughter, and we gravitate to people who make us laugh. Our relationships are stronger if laughter is part of them. Men and women both agree that the ability to make them laugh is one of the most attractive traits they look for in a prospective suitor. We love to laugh together because it lightens our emotional load and refreshes our energy. If a shared good laugh makes our skin tingle, imagine how it's impacting the resonance of our energetic field and that of the other person's. We must light up like the aurora borealis.

Because of the high personal engagement necessary to laugh, it also enhances team spirit. The more our families, businesses and communities share laughter, the more resilient the team becomes. It's the ultimate leadership tool which many of our country leaders could employ more frequently.

The simple act of pulling our lips up and showing our teeth, crinkling the skin around the corners of our eyes and putting a twinkle in them relays the message to our brain that it's time to laugh and the happy drugs kick in. When we do this socially, laughter become spontaneous. A jolly good laugh reduces the need for pharmaceutical therapy; headaches disappear, and pain is noticeably relieved.

You may say there's not a lot in the world worth laughing about. Yet we're all responsible for being the fun and laughter we seek in our lives. It's not up to anyone else to make us laugh or be happy.

If we're serious about happiness, (pun intended) we can get this energy moving by approaching life with a childlike attitude. Young children look for the wonder in their lives and seek out the best in their world. They experience every day and everything as if for *the first time*, not the last time. Filled with wonder, not only do they look for magic, they expect magic to happen to them. When children play, they allow life to unfold around them, reveling in the joyousness each day brings, eager for the next experience. Oftentimes the joy that we, as adults, experience while watching children at play, is a remembrance of our own innocence and childlike attitude. It's a recollection of the inherent playfulness we long to express once more.

As children, before we're conditioned by our limited human perspective, being playful was the key methodology by which we experienced our world. Through play we dared to stand and walk. We laughed spontaneously and joyously at our first failed attempts when we fell before picking ourselves up to start over again.

Since playfulness, spontaneity and joy act as positive-energy transmitters, we need to add more to our lives. Watching funny movies, TV shows, or YouTube videos, making funny videos, reading funny books or having a dress-up games night at home is a start. We can spend time goofing around with the children, playing with the pet or doing something silly just for the hell of it.

Once social distancing is over, be sure to keep laughter in your day and don't fall into the trap of endlessly discussing the pandemic. Go to laughter yoga or a laughter wellness class, catch up with friends and share funny stories or support a local comedy club. Whatever you do, laugh.

Like the coronavirus, laughter is contagious. But unlike the virus, the more we spread it around, the better. Laughter needs no vaccine because it's already the best medicine.

Life is what we make.

Love is what enriches it.

And laughter keeps us well.

EXERCISE:

Research and list ten comedies you'll watch during isolation. Give each a laughter rating after watching them.

1. _____

2. _____

3. _____

4. _____

5. _____

6. _____

7. _____

8. _____

9. _____

10. _____

Watch Mary Poppins (the original 1964 version with Julie Andrews) paying attention to the scene where they take tea on the ceiling, 'I love to laugh'.

List some fun activities you'll do to add more laughter to your life now and once social distancing has been lifted.

We are at a unique stage in our history.
Never before have we had such an awareness of what we are doing to the planet and never before have we had the power to do something about that.
Surely we all have a responsibility to care for our Blue Planet.
The future of humanity and indeed, all life on earth, now depends on us."

Sir David Attenborough

NINETEEN

Our Precious Planet

Genesis 1:28 talks about man's place in the world and states ... *and have dominion over the fish of the sea, and over the fowl of the air, and over every living thing that moveth upon the earth.* Note the word is dominion—not domination, destruction or desecration. Dominion implies sovereignty with wise counsel, whereas we've taken on the role of tyrant, an autocratic despot. As a species we've relinquished our caretaker role and instead of being guardians of our precious planet, we've become its jailer and in many cases, its torturer.

For generations, young people have marched, protested and demanded change. The passionate plea of the young to save our planet is not a new phenomenon. Though many today would think it's their private domain. Over the past decades, some positive change has happened, but it's still markedly little, considering the level of technology we have at our disposal to facilitate change.

Despite the heated debates, the diametrically

opposed research and obdurate stands for and against, one truth prevails, but is rarely considered. *Everything is energy* and this includes our planet. Every aspect is Consciousness in expression, resonating at different frequencies, holding the cohesive patterns we label as plants, animals, oceans, mountains and deserts. Even if we disregard the scientific and existential proof of its existence, everything resonates at its own electromagnetic frequency energizing the planet and everything that depends on it for life. The planets, the solar system, the universe and all there is in the cosmos is made of the same stuff. It's all infinite, intelligent Consciousness expressing itself uniquely. *We are all the same*.

Then why has humanity continued in its disrespect, contempt and ruination of our home? The many reasons have long been debated, but there's one underlying motive why we've perpetrated such abuse on the planet and its inhabitants, human and animal. Because most of humanity still believes it's separate. Separate from each other, separate from the environment, separate from the animals, and most importantly separate from themselves, their *being*.

Unlike ants where the colony works as one, we have worshipped at the altar of individuality and independence for so long that we've squandered the greater good for individual gain. And while we sit in control at the top of the food chain, believing in the separateness of everything, we're able to justify and continue this carnage. As Simon Wiesenthal so eloquently wrote, "For evil to flourish, it only requires good men to do nothing."

So, as 'good men', what can we do to support the environment? We can commit to using our isolation wisely, to researching and investigating different viewpoints relating to the planet. We can become self-educated by means of external information and our inner resources. Though self-education is gaining mainstream momentum, it'll be self-knowing gained from personal transformation that will be the litmus test. No longer content to be told and expected to follow blindly, we want to *know*. Our kids are teaching us that!

As a family, we can help the environment by reducing, reusing and recycling, conserving water, choosing products based on how they're sourced and manufactured, reducing our meat intake and moving to vegetarianism, minimizing plastic packaging, planting a tree and signing online petitions such as the closure of all live animal meat markets across the world. Additionally, if the rate of deforestation is anything to go by, particularly in the Amazon, our atmosphere will be loaded with carbon not just because of escalating carbon emissions but because the planet's lungs will have been decimated.

It's time to respect all creatures as sentient beings. They're not here to be hunted, tortured or brutalized because we're consumed by ego and ignorance. Animals have feelings, are highly intuitive and are our energetic companions. Studies show many species respond to and appreciate music, others have keen psychic abilities like dogs knowing when their owners are returning home and many visibly mourn the loss of one of their family group. It's up to each of us to respect, love and appreciate their presence in our lives and the planet, for how we treat them is how we will be treated. Cruelty and brutality always come home to roost. What we sow, so shall we reap.

As Mahatma Ghandi wrote, "The greatness of a nation and its moral progress can be judged by the way its animals are treated. I hold that the more helpless a creature the more entitled it is to protection by man from the cruelty of humankind."

We must teach our children to be kind to all animals, for only then will they learn to be kind to each other. Once more, we stand at the brink of global change, hopefully more aware and attuned as a species than before. Maybe this time, a powerful grass roots movement to reenergize the planet will finally gather momentum and find voice.

Let's return to the analogy of the ant. Consider that we're the workers, going about our business to keep the colony thriving, while the queen, Mother Earth relays the plans to us through Nature's blueprint. Our role is to connect to the group consciousness and ensure we follow the blueprint for the greater good of the colony, the greater good for the planet.

But you say, there are many workers who don't do that. They're corrupt, deceitful and ignorant. This is true because as humans we have free will. The freedom to choose to live from a limited human perspective or to shift to a love-based Master Mindset. There will always be those who choose for the ego, but we must never forget that we're all one Consciousness. Our role isn't to judge or blame another worker. Our role is to keep the colony alive.

What we have on our side is wisdom. We *know* we have power in our group consciousness. The Maharishi Effect study proved it. One of the least discussed ways to revive our planet is through mass meditation, mass energetic channeling for a common outcome. It's happening now with global hope meditations prompted by the pandemic. People everywhere are meditating and praying in the thousands, tens of thousands, probably millions for a common purpose. Why not for the planet?

If everyone who meditates, held the image of a healthy, thriving planet in their minds and focused on its flourishing forests, clean oceans and waterways, safe animals and radical laws being passed for the planet's intelligent governance, a new reality would emerge. It will require patience, but we know the power of the mind is limitless. Where many gather in the name of peace, of Consciousness, they make it so. That's not to say, that those whose mission it is to take massive action to halt environmental destruction shouldn't fulfill their purpose. But it's the strategic head and not the hot head that triumphs in the end. Fear, blame and anger will only lead to more hostility which will manifest in covert destruction.

Generational finger-pointing, no matter how selfless the intention, will do little to expedite change. Real change comes from within the individual. And how best to demonstrate this but through our personal realities. When we shift to a Maser Mindset and create extraordinary results in our own lives and businesses, others will want to know how we did it, and in their transformation, global change will accelerate through the Consciousness.

This was illustrated in the hundredth monkey experiment back in the 1950's on the island of Koshima. Researchers performed studies of the local population of monkeys by dumping sweet potatoes on the beach. This particular species of monkey had never encountered sweet potatoes before and, while they liked the vegetable, they didn't like the sandy coating. Then one monkey genius discovered she could clean the potatoes by washing them in the sea. First a few other monkeys, observing this, did the same and then others followed. Then suddenly the entire troop took to washing their potatoes. But then a strange phenomenon occurred. Researchers on a faraway island observed their monkeys using the same washing technique. The conclusion was that the information acquired by a certain number of any given species acts like flashpoint and is relayed via the group consciousness.

In this era of acceleration, we each have a part to play, and like the monkeys and the ants, we each have impact. We *are* necessary to the whole. Our every thought, perception, belief, value, emotion, feeling, word and action influences the energy. The more we focus this energy to revealing our *being*, and the earth's inherent wholeness, the faster we'll save this precious planet.

EXERCISE:

In the below article from the World Economic Forum 2018, Marco Lambertini, Director-General, WWF International summarizes the planet's health.

In just over 40 years, the world has witnessed 60% decline in wildlife populations across land, sea and freshwater and is heading towards a shocking fall of two-thirds by 2020. This has happened in less than two generations. Forests are under pressure like never before, through unabated deforestation. 170 million hectares of additional deforestation will occur by 2030 – the size of Mongolia – driven by large-and small-scale livestock farming and soy and palm oil production. Our oceans are under great stress. We dump plastic and toxic chemicals into the sea, poisoning our own food. We catch fish wastefully and unsustainably, with 90% of the world's fish stocks overfished. We've lost 50% of the world's coral reefs in the last 30 years. In a generation, the world has lost nearly half of its marine species populations. The last five years have been the warmest five-year period on record, while the Arctic warmed much faster than predicted and the UN estimates that, in the last 10 years, climate-related disasters have caused $1.4 trillion of damage worldwide.

Consider which of these or other environmental issues gives you the deepest visceral sensation of distress?

_____
_____
_____

Take a few minutes now to visualize the remedy for this issue. Engage your five senses and send out the positive image of rejuvenation and reconstruction. Know that the energy you experience for environmental healing is making an impact. Commit to including this in your daily meditations.

Afterwards, research this issue and decide how you can further affect positive change for the planet.

How can share your new environmental awareness with your family and how can you work together to make a difference?

**Imagine all the people
Livin' life in a world of peace**

John Lennon

TWENTY

We are One

In fundamental terms when we live with a Master Mindset, we know the true sequence of life is being, doing and having. We've given up the limited human perspective of trying to live in the reverse order of having, doing and being. We no longer believe that *having* what we want and *doing* what we want, will ever lead us to *being* the fullest expression of who we came here to be. We know that who we're *being* sets the vibrational resonance of our Consciousness.

We appreciate that we're Consciousness with a body and that we have access to the wisdom of that Consciousness every moment of every day. We engage our inner resources through faith and trust, through peace, meditation and intuition, and through our imagination, creativity and inspiration. We empower ourselves with certainty by taking responsibility for all aspects of our health by making conscious decisions, practicing active gratitude and aligning with a future focus. And we energize ourselves through affirmations and actions and live consciously committed to resonating at the purest frequency of Consciousness. We live from *being* as a verb, not a noun. And it's from this deep experience of peace that love and compassion grow. A love that is detached from ego and is willing to see all things brand new, including each other.

Because of our long-held belief of separateness and our ego-centric perspective, each of us still struggle with yielding to the Truth about loving each other. Sure, it's easy to love them if she has the same values as me, or he likes the same things as me, or their view on life is like mine. But it's a lot harder to love her if she lives on the streets or he's cruel to his dog or they worship a God I don't believe in. The ego places conditions on our love, distorting our resonant frequency and blocking the flow of energy to and from our lives. Our reality becomes less about love and more about fear.

Still, our *being* is love twenty-four hours a day whether we acknowledge it or not. And since everything is energy, and we're all one Consciousness, this is true for everyone. Even for the despots, the murderers, the wife beaters and pedophiles. Most of us rail at the thought, much preferring to shame, blame and judge these societal misfits. But love is universal, the purest resonant energy of all. Just because we love, doesn't mean we condone.

In our resolute refusal to allow violent or criminal deeds to persist, we must also know that the unacceptable action alone doesn't identify the true essence of the perpetrator. We can't change their reality or their perspective, but we can entrust them to their *being.* That is love. We must dare to register the Truth, and if individual and collective transformation are what we seek, then we must be willing to love. For without love, there can be no lasting change.

Layer after layer, the pandemic is peeling back our limited human perspective. Social contact, playing with friends, visiting family, going to church, shopping and the demise of life as we knew it has been stripped from us. In our involuntary isolation, we've been exposed. There's nowhere to hide. No work, no gatherings, no occasions, no outings, no beach, no gym. There's nowhere to run to take our mind off the incessant restlessness caused by the ego. Love and fear stand before us clearer than ever before. Which bedfellow do we choose? Are we willing to see the Truth in ourselves and each other? Or will we cower under the pillow and hope the nightmare will end? Yet in the final analysis, we inherently know that love and peace are critical to healing ourselves and the world.

The act of giving love is the fastest, most direct route to the heart of humanity and to healing the planet. Whether or not the other person receives our love mustn't influence our willingness to love. We must forgive others not because they deserve it, but because the world deserves peace. Despite the outcome, the love we give makes energetic deposits in a universal bank and changes the world. Love is never wasted.

If we consider love, we eventually recognize a simple truth—when we love another, we're loving our *being*. The other reflects our own radiance, Consciousness and immortality. Like a mirror, they shine with all good, all light, all godliness and we respond in kind. Everything and everyone in our world become brand new because we're willing to give love, receive love and be loved.

We spontaneously act with caring, responsibility, respect, humility, intimacy, courage, honesty, vulnerability and commitment with the intention of creating pleasure, security, safety and trust for the other. In truth, love is the willingness to recognize infinite, intelligent Consciousness in each and everything.

With love, we no longer blame or shame ourselves or others. We no longer grasp for excuses for our actions. When we love, we no longer play the victim or the martyr, or feel guilty or do whatever we please with no regard for others.

The selfish mantra of "What's in it for me?" shifts to "How do I serve the greater good?" Aspiring to help others and being someone of value elevates our decision making and aligns us with our purpose. Energetically, it enhances our well-being and those we love. Even if we're not currently in the position to be of service in a major way, we can be of service for the greater good by our daily commitment to love a little bit more. What greater service can we give to humanity than to love. Until we're willing to be of value and of service to others, very little of value will manifest in our lives.

With love, we no longer see the world as a hostile place with killer viruses trying to infect us. We know that it's not more protection we need. It's love, not just for the coronavirus patients but for everyone. For the cancer patients who will die sooner because their treatments are being delayed because of the attention being given to the virus. For the millions of children who die in anonymity each year from starvation. For the countless species going extinct, and for the guy who cuts us off in traffic.

Love isn't for one and not the other. Love is for all. When we dare to be undefended against the greater good and love each other, we experience *being*, individually and collectively.

It is love that enriches the evolution of human Consciousness.

And with love, we will rise above!

EXERCISE:

Do you act with caring, responsibility, respect, humility, intimacy, courage, honesty, vulnerability and commitment with the intention of creating pleasure, security, safety and trust for another? List three situations that demonstrate this.

_____
_____
_____
_____
_____
_____
_____
_____

Ask yourself, "How can I serve the greater good?" and write your answers here.

_____
_____
_____
_____
_____
_____
_____

Embody, enact and energize each of your actions, building momentum and resonance.

**Somewhere over the rainbow, bluebirds fly,
and the dreams that you dare to dream
really do come true.**

Israel Kamakawiwoʻole

TWENTY-ONE

Mastering a Brighter Future

And this brings us full circle to the initial question, "Who are you *being*?"

Resist the ego's urge to project into the future by asking disempowering questions such as "Who am I *going to be*?" or "What am I *going to do*?" or "What will I *have* left?" when social distancing has been relaxed and life gets back to some semblance of normalcy. We can never do anything in time and space. Only in the instant. The only moment we live in is the present. If we try to project and make decisions in the future we'll end up making ourselves sick from worry. The solution to every problem lies in aligning with *being* and letting Consciousness deal with it, instead of trying to sort it out ourselves. We must persevere in doing the only thing which interrupts thinking—align with *being* and listen for guidance.

The sooner we move to the final stage in the grief process of graceful acceptance that life will never be the same again, the easier it will be. We can never go back.

It's a natural law of the universe that once growth begins, momentum carries it forward. And growth has definitely begun. For some, it's growth of fear. Hopefully for you, it's growth of faith that everything is right time, right place and works for me.

We have the choice to be like the butterfly and yield into our transformation, trusting that we're being taken care of. We can surrender to the changes happening within us, dare to *be* more and master our lives. Then after our transformation, we'll emerge more elegant, loving and peaceful, possessed of powers we never knew we had before we went into isolation. Like the butterfly, we'll be equipped to fly somewhere over the rainbow.

Looking back wistfully to the 'good old days before the pandemic' lowers the resonance of our Consciousness, whereas the vision of a brighter future exudes enormous drawing power. It energizes our life and attracts to us that which is 'the best is yet to come'. The present moment is the gift in which challenges and opportunities abound as offerings for us to master our destiny. When we become more conscious of being Consciousness in expression, the parts of our lives which appeared to be lacking are reversed, healed and changed.

Mastery is to give, receive and be loved right in the face of madness and adversity. It's allowing the world of circumstances and conditions to do its little jig while we remain in the peaceful space of *being*. We must each dare to step beyond our limited, human perspective, in order to experience a new frame of reference, so we can master our lives.

Life is meant to be easy, but we make it hard by viewing it through the lens of the limited human perspective. Imagine your life as a large, furnished room filled with exquisite pieces of furniture and decorated with expensive soft furnishings. It's exactly as you dreamed it. Every piece in its place, waiting for you to enjoy it. Except there's no light. The room is in total darkness. You can't see anything as you stand at the threshold and you become anxious. "What happened to the light?"

Your fear rises. Perhaps there's something sinister lurking in the dark ready to attack you. The fear prickles your skin. But you want to go in. It's *your* room. It belongs to *you*. How dare someone turn off the lights! Finally, you summon up the courage to step inside but stub your toe on unseen furniture. Damn! It hurts. "Wait until you find out who did this to you. They'll pay the price."

You retreat, limping to the threshold, where you rub your toe and curse your life. For years, you stand at the darkened doorway of your destiny, fearful, pitiful and angry, looking into the blackness trying to work out what went wrong. Why is it so dark?

And then one day, you shift your perspective, away from the problem to the solution. You know inherently there must be light somewhere and a distant memory inspires you to run your hand up and down the threshold. Your fingers rest on something. You're not quite sure what it is. Maybe it will kill you. Maybe it will save you. It's a switch. And herein lies your power. An energetic power beyond measure. Though still unsure, you have faith that this is the answer you've been searching for. You flick the switch.

And like magic, your life lights up and you're awestruck by its magnificence. It's even more beautiful and bountiful than you imagined. It's then you realize how easy it really was. You'd been anguishing all that time over nothing. All you needed to do was make a shift of perspective, have faith and flick the switch to power up the light. And the same applies to each of us. When we power up our energetic frequency with love, compassion and faith, we become enlightened. The brighter our resonance, the brighter the future we attract.

Consciousness is life-affirming and life-supporting, and if we are to master a brighter future, we must reaffirm this through our thoughts, perceptions, beliefs, values, words, actions and habits.

It's easy to feel good.
It's easy to be who I am.
It's easy to get a job.
It's easy to build a new life.
My life feels good, real, comfortable, true and loving.

Resonating at this frequency sets the vibrational tone for a matching reality to manifest in our lives. This energy primes us for our post-pandemic life, and like an empty vessel, we become infilled with extraordinary results.

Still, you might catch yourself nervously projecting into the future, worrying about a job or your livelihood. This is the time to consider Leonardo Da Vinci's advice. "Study the science of art. Study the art of science.

Develop your senses—especially learn how to see. Realize that everything connects to everything else."

Right now, and for the foreseeable future, it pays to be a polymath, a person of wide knowledge. Use this time to hone new skills, new interests, become the best at one thing or very good at two or more things. Explore multiple disciplines. Add more strings to your proverbial bow of learning. Pay attention to what you're guided to do and where to go. And most importantly, don't trade time for regrets.

In the final analysis, the fundamental question still remains…

Who *are you being*?

Right now!

For those of us who dare to fling our dreams, visions and destiny out into Consciousness with the faith to know and claim it as our own, we will find it is done.

EXERCISE:

Answer the below questions based on your present moment experience.

Who am I *being?*

_____
_____
_____
_____
_____
_____
_____

What am I focusing on?

_____
_____
_____
_____
_____
_____
_____

What do things mean to me?

_____
_____
_____
_____
_____
_____
_____

What am I going to do about them?

___

If I knew I couldn't fail, what would I do to improve the world?

___

If I was going to die one year from today, what would I do to serve the greater good before I died?

___

Live life as if everything is rigged in your favor.

Rumi

Wearing the Crown

Since the dawn of man, religious faiths have long prophesied the end of days. Some are waiting for the Judgement Day, others for Armageddon, some await the Messiah while others wait for the Second Coming of Christ. Yet all agree it will be a time when humanity will be held accountable for their actions. If this was such a time, would we be joyously accountable or shamefully embarrassed? Have we served the greater good?

In a way, our forced isolation is the end of days of our previous lives. A time to take stock and be accountable for our actions. A time when fundamental questions need to be asked and a new blueprint for humanity developed.

Do we want our new world order to be one where money is valued over integrity? Now that we've been forced to reassess our own lives, we recognize the value of peace, love and compassion. In getting to know our children better, can we continue turning a blind eye to the child sex trafficking market? Can we continue to trade with companies and countries with horrific human and animal rights records? When we buy our groceries, are we going to buy cheaper products rather than spending a little extra to support sustainable and organic farming methods? Is cheaper always best when it comes to choosing between our hip pocket and backing our local growers or ethically manufactured products? Each of us must decide where money and integrity rank in the value hierarchy of our lives. We must make a conscious choice and take massive consistent action to demonstrate the change we expect. We can't sit in judgement and blame governments, if we're reneging at the check-out.

Do we want our new world to be one where fear is valued over truth? How long will we tolerate organizations peddling fear? Many media outlets scandalize information under the banner of news without any thought as to the impact this has on people's lives. Sure, we have the freedom to turn it off and the more we exercise that freedom, the sooner programming will change. But what about the elderly who've come to rely on the news, still believing it's the truth. They are being fed a diet of fear in pursuit of ratings. Real truth is never inflamed by opinion, nor slanted by politics, nor presented to terrify and vilify. We must master our devices, turn off the fear, the blame and the ridicule and demand positive, enriching programming. And if we can't change the business model of these and other like-minded fear-mongering organizations, we can change what we allow in our homes and in our minds.

Do we want our new world to be one of separateness or oneness? Though we know everything is energy and that we're all one Consciousness, are we going to live with love from this Truth? Every time we act with love, compassion, kindness, respect, generosity and integrity we heal ourselves and each other from the misguided belief of separateness. When we serve another without putting our selfish gain first, we heal. When we give to the homeless instead of turning away, we heal. When we dare to be defenseless with each other, we heal. And when we make peace with our past, forgive and choose love, we heal.

In the end, what type of world do we want our children to inherit? One of panic or peace.

The ultimate is happening now. It's our perspective which makes it good or bad, right or wrong. But there is no duality, only Consciousness. From a distance, we are ants scurrying around trying not to lose too many workers as we try to save our colony. But we're no match for the law of natural selection. It is what it is. The best we can do is align with the unfoldment of our *being* and know that the Truth will indeed set us free from the panic, the fear and the dis-ease.

When we consider life from this context, we must question if the name of the coronavirus is a coincidence? Corona means crown. From a Master Mindset, we'd view this as a significant omen that humanity is entering a new age of sovereignty. Not over others but over ignorance. A new age of evolving human Consciousness not just in scattered clusters, but collectively.

Part of evolution is attributed to viruses which can

transfer from organism to organism, speeding up the evolutionary process through random mutation. Perhaps the coronavirus is necessary for the awakening of human Consciousness. Those who are ready to shift to a higher frequency are unaffected, while those with vibrationally dense energies opt out. Could the code being inserted by the coronavirus be the link to the purest frequency of Consciousness? Maybe we *are* awakening from the dream that we've slept so long. The struggle between staying asleep and waking up is at once, scary and enlivening. But as always, the choice of the experience is ours.

In the end, there is only one thing for sure. Everyone feels it. There is a surge of energy, of power rising. And as sovereign over our lives, we must respect the sovereignty of others. We must all wear the crown that fits and build a global society for the greater good.

There is a pattern of Consciousness which is eternal, indestructible and as changeless as Truth, manifesting through us in perfect form. It is an immutable, universal law giving each of us the irresistible urge to live more fully. We can either accept or reject this urge.

Who will you *be* in the brave new world?

Sovereign or slave.

If you'd like to know more about developing a Master Mindset and living a life that matters, take Diane's Mindset Mastery Assessment at
https://mastermindset.com.au/assessment/

For daily inspiration, join Diane on
www.facebook.com/groups/shiftinghumanperspective

For more information, go to
https://dianedemetre.com/

Follow her on
https://www.facebook.com/DianeDemetreOfficial
OR https://www.instagram.com/dianedemetreofficial

AWARD WINNING AUTHOR

> " . . . Dare to dream bigger than ever before, dare to forge your own path no matter how hard the challenges. But most of all, dare to *be* you and let the chips fall where they may. We are all warrior women with gossamer wings . . . It's time to soar!"
>
> — Diane Demetre

Winner of 2019 SBAA International Women's Day Leader Award for Leadership in the Entertainment, Creative Arts and/or Media Industry.

Diane was nominated as a finalist in the ARRA Awards 2018 for Favourite Romantic Suspense, for her novel *Retribution*.

In 2017, Diane won the Romance Writers of Australia Emerald Pro Award for Best Unpublished Romance Manuscript, for her novel *Retribution*.

Also by Diane Demetre

Diane Demetre is an award-winning author of contemporary, genre-busting romance, suspense and mystery novels including:

Killer in the Outback

Evil on the High Seas

Island of Secrets

Retribution

Take Me

Teach Me

Tempt Me

Further Notes

Further Notes

Further Notes

Further Notes

Further Notes

www.ingramcontent.com/pod-product-compliance
Lightning Source LLC
Chambersburg PA
CBHW030255010526
44107CB00053B/1720

9780648332480